Jake Bernstein's

FACTS ON FUTURES

Insights and Strategies for Winning in the Futures Markets

by
JAKE BERNSTEIN

PROBUS PUBLISHING COMPANY
Chicago, Illinois

© JACOB BERNSTEIN, 1987

Library of Congress Cataloging-in-Publication Data

Bernstein, Jacob.
　　Jake Bernstein's facts on futures.

　　Bibliography: p.
　　Includes index.
　　1. Financial futures.　I. Title.　II. Title:
Facts on futures.
HG6024.3.B47　1986　　332.64'4　　86-12214
ISBN 0-917253-44-2

Library of Congress Catalog Card No. 86-12214

Printed in the United States of America

1　2　3　4　5　6　7　8　9　0

ACKNOWLEDGEMENTS

I wish to extend a note of special thanks (not necessarily in order of importance) to the following organizations and individuals:

Commodity Quote Graphics for permission to use charts from their excellent computer quotation system; R. Earl Hadaday and Martin Weiss for permission to use charts from their various publications; Intermarket Magazine for permission to quote extensively from their Tom Baldwin and J. Peter Steidlmayer interviews; Probus Publishing; Interface Studios for an excellent and appealing type-setting job; and, of course, Marilyn Kinney who runs my office, for her input which is always useful but not always immediately appreciated.

"The truth does not become more true by virtue of the fact that the entire world agrees with it, nor less so even if the whole world disagrees with it."

Moreh Nevuchim 2:15

Table of Contents

Preface

The futures renaissance was officially born in 1982 when stock index futures were approved for trading by the Securities and Exchange Commission and the Commodity Futures Trading Commission. Until the early 1980s futures trading was seen by many as a gamble, a high-stakes speculation game, a crap shoot, or worse. The investing public was taught to shun futures trading by a brokerage community indoctrinated by over 100 years of trading in stocks and bonds. Notwithstanding the sad state of the individual investor, securities brokers continued to recommend their pet vehicles to the public as the "best" way to accumulate wealth . . . "the good old-fashioned way."

As the three-piece suited stock brokers sat on suburban commuter trains headed to town, the less formally attired futures brokers had already been in their offices for several hours trading in foreign currency and Eurodollar futures, T bond and T bill futures and precious metal futures. By the time the Big Board opened, literally hundreds of millions of dollars worth of futures contracts had already changed hands. While the price of memberships on the New York Stock Exchange made a slow and steady slide from high hundreds of thousands of dollars to the low hundreds of thousands of dollars, cost of memberships on futures exchanges was quickly increasing by thousands of percent. While futures brokerage houses were reaping immense profits, security brokerage firms were pinching pennies, laying off staff, and silently studying the unorthodox thing called "futures trading."

Then, through the wisdom of the various government regulatory agencies and extreme pressure of brokerage house lobbyists, futures trading in stock index futures was approved. Though not readily understood or employed by many investors and speculators, trading in these new vehicles slowly gained in popularity, and when the bull market in stocks gained momentum in 1982, stock index trading increased dramatically. Suddenly old-line securities firms were recommending stock index futures to their customers and within a matter of months, trading in all types of futures contracts had gained considerable public approval and was, for the first time in many years, "respectable." It took the hybridization of stocks and futures to make futures more palatable to the brokerage house and investment community. Futures trading in such vehicles as T bonds, T bills, foreign currencies, commercial paper, T notes, GNMAs and Eurodollars also participated in the futures renaissance.

Today, as futures trading continues to grow in popularity, there are new vehicles designed to capture the attention of traders and investors. Trading in futures options has added another new dimension to the variety of tools and vehicles by which the speculator and/or investor can capitalize on price swings. It is now possible to limit the risk one takes on futures positions by buying or selling an option on a futures contract. If this all sounds too confusing, too esoteric, too intricate; if the world of futures trading seems too obscure to command your attention; if you're tempted to hide your head in the sand in order to avoid futures...then this is the book for you! Today more than ever before, it is vital for all investors to understand futures, their workings, the meaning of futures price trends, and the manner in which trading in the various futures vehicles can benefit a total investment portfolio. Futures and options trading strategies allow for combinations and **actions** never before available to investors.

It is the purpose of this book to educate all investors and potential investors in futures and futures options trading in a fashion that departs from the traditional approaches taken in teaching this subject. There is little emphasis on history, economic justification, controversial issues, and the hazards of futures trading. The many tax ramifications and strategies are given only passing attention. The manner in which futures trading is used as a means of hedging risk is given only brief attention. All of these topics have been adequately and abundantly covered in the past. Virtually every public library is overstocked with books discussing these aspects of futures trading. However, I do not believe that the public has ever been offered an opportunity to learn futures and options on a very basic and nontheoretical level.

In effect, the book you are about to read, *is a layman's guide to futures and options. It seeks to provide you with the information you will need to get started and it will help you determine whether you, in fact, want to get started.* It will help you learn if futures and futures options trading are right for you, and if you decide that they are, this book will provide you with the direction you will need to learn more. Even the experienced trader will find this book helpful as a refresher course or quick reference guide. My goal is, first and foremost, to educate the public in an area of finance that has for too long received either unfavorable or incomplete attention.

Finally, and on a more general level, my goal is teach investors that they must, at the very minimum, understand futures trading since futures price trends tend to forecast or predict economic direction. It is not my intention to sell anyone on the virtues of futures trading. I do believe, however, that a good understanding of futures and the meaning of futures price movements can be very beneficial in understanding, forecasting, and anticipating economic direction and change. I believe that it is the mandate of every investor who claims to be well-rounded and informed to understand the workings of the futures market and, above all, to understand how changes in futures prices tend to precede changes in other sectors of the economy.

AUTHOR'S NOTE

To write a worthwhile book on a subject as complex and mul-
tifaceted as futures trading is indeed a difficult undertaking. So
many things should be covered that cannot be, and so many things
should be covered in great detail but, unfortunately, can only be
covered in general terms. Those who master this book (and I have
made this task relatively simple) are encouraged to expand their
understanding by pursuing further studies in the areas I have,
through limited space, been forced to cover only briefly.

My varied experiences with futures trading since 1968 have
taught me many valuable lessons. The things I have learned by
trial and error are more clearly valuable than any lessons based
exclusively on the study and/or memorization of strictly pedagog-
ical material. The *facts* of futures trading are available virtually
anywhere; many excellent books will tell you what you ought to
know. There are, however, precious few books that will give you
information that transcends facts and turns theory into practice;
practice into results.

In writing this book, I was faced with an agonizing choice.
Should I attempt to make my mark as a thorough, knowledge-
able, and articulate teacher of futures market facts, or should I
attempt to achieve a much more meaningful goal, namely that of
instilling in the reader a sixth sense or experiential background,
which is much more valuable than facts alone can ever be. The
pros and cons of each approach were, indeed, numerous. To produce a strictly factual book would have been a relatively simple
undertaking. All that would have been required of me was to spend
many hours at my dictation machine and/or at my typewriter,
spewing forth a wealth of factual information that I have acquired
through the years. Of course, I would have presented the information in my own particular fashion attempting to imbue the
reader with the pragmatics and techniques designed to make the

facts useful. The result would have been an especially large man-
uscript covering literally hundreds of subjects, containing numerous illustrations, and probably losing most readers to boredom
after the first several chapters.

My book would then have joined the ranks of the so many
general, frequently boring and often poorly written texts on the
futures markets. To add to my list of achievements something of
such a nature, something which has already been done perhaps
better than I could ever do it, would not be something about which
I could be especially proud. However, to do something that has
not been done before—to make my mark in an area attempted
by few; to produce a work of rich meaning that would survive
for years to come—that was something that most certainly attracted
and held my attention.

Unfortunately, the disadvantages of such an approach had to
be considered, as well. What were some of the disadvantages I
envisioned? First and foremost a book such as the one I intended
to write, must, by its very nature, stray from the beaten path. To
stray from the beaten path certainly leaves one open to ridicule.
Naturally, some would agree with what I planned to say, but I knew
that some would take strong exception to the concepts and asser-
tions I planned to present. The risk, however, did not concern me,
since no great reward is possible without risk.

In closing this preamble I will leave you with a number of
thoughts, all near and dear to my heart. To avoid having these
thoughts camouflaged in the text of my explanations, I will
innumerate them regardless of how unromantic that may be.

1. *Futures trading is not a science.* No matter how, when or with
   what degree of intensity and effort you try to confine futures
   trading to mechanical models, scientific procedures and operational techniques, you cannot totally relegate speculation in
   futures to a mechanistic methodology that will filter out the
   human element.
2. Because of this, *any book that purports to present futures trading
   as a pure science, or as a form of technological perfection, is missing the entire point* of speculation itself.

3. *Futures trading is as much an art as it is a science;* as much a game of guts as it is a game of brains.
4. *Facts are no more or less important than techniques.* Techniques reside more within the realm of art than in the realm of science. In today's age of computer technology, we have taught machines to do everything from speaking to drawing. Yet, we do not have machines that will produce true works of art, works that will be cherished for centuries to come. Perhaps one day we will have computers that can produce such works of art in the style of the masters, but that day is not today.
5. *This book teaches techniques,* imparts experience, provides direction, emphasizes methodology and fills the gap between knowledge and achievement.

Facts and "book learning" are what you seek, then do not read this book. I can refer you to countless other texts that will give you precisely what you want. If, however, the ability to put facts into action is what you truly seek, then this is indeed the book for you! Perhaps you will find my explanations and interpretations at times to be unconventional or even radical. It is, perhaps, my many years experience, shaped and developed in all types of markets since 1968, that have made me the skeptic and iconoclast I am.

Jake Bernstein

Prologue

An Introduction to Futures and Futures Options

For many years futures trading has been considered either too risky or too sophisticated for the average investor. Most myths are born of ignorance and the futures myth is no exception. For all too long, futures trading was either ignored or shunned in economics texts and, as a consequence, the general public was not educated in the basics of futures. No informed choice could, therefore, be made.

Investments in securities (i.e., stocks, bonds and even stock options), however, received considerable attention since they were more traditional. It is generally believed that trading in stocks has more historical justification and, therefore, more value in an economic education. There are, in addition, a number of other reasons for the historically diminutive role of futures trading.

Before launching into an explanation of precisely what futures trading is, it may be necessary to "clear the decks" of any misconceptions you may hold. Therefore, let's first examine some of the standard objections to futures trading, so that we may have a relatively clean slate upon which to write the new learning. Generally, objections to futures trading fall into several categories, all based on either partial or distorted facts. Let's take a look at a few of these misconceptions as expressed by contemporary stereotypical statements.

1. **"You Can Lose All You've Invested, or More, if You Trade in Futures."**

   This is true. However, the key word is *invested*. Trading futures should in no way, shape, or form be considered an investment. As a *speculation*, however, the rules of the game become distinctly different—high risk is necessary for high reward. Nevertheless, even "high risk" does not mean that the common sense rules of good trading (to be taught in this book) should be ignored.

2. **"Trading in Futures Is a Gamble."**

   This is another misconception. In fact, trading in futures is technically and fundamentally no different from trading in stocks. The odds of being right or wrong are essentially similar. However, due to lower margins, the odds of making money in futures are probably lower than those of making money in stocks. Ultimately, the possible percentage return in futures trading is considerably greater than the potential return in stocks. Futures trading is, therefore, not any more of a gamble than trading in stocks. Carefully and closely following the rules of successful futures trading will help reduce the risk and gamble.

3. **"Futures Trading Is for Insiders . . . It's a 'Rigged' Game."**

   These two misconceptions go hand in hand. There is probably less "inside" information available in futures than there is in the stock market. The United States Department of Agriculture, the Commodity Futures Trading Commission and the National Futures Association have imposed very stringent limits on the total number of positions a trader may hold. They monitor the brokerage industry and large trader transactions very closely. Important government information is guarded and kept strictly secret until the scheduled release date and time. In this way, the markets can function freely and with minimal effects of insider information. Unavoidably, some traders will always have an edge based on inside information, but success in the futures market is very possible without access to such information.

4. **"Trading in Futures Serves No Economic Purpose ...It's Pure Speculation."**
This popular misconception couldn't be farther from the truth. The futures markets serve to stabilize prices. Speculators are often willing to take market positions when prices are fluctuating significantly due to news, weather, crop conditions, etc. This stabilizes prices by providing additional buyers and sellers to buffer extreme moves. Were it not for the speculator, prices would move more viciously than they presently do. Were it not for speculators buying and selling regardless of price levels, the markets would be subject to great volatility. Supplies would stand a good chance of being disrupted as they are in communist and socialist economies.

5. **"Futures Trading Is Only for the Short Term."**
This is also incorrect. Futures trading can be either long term, intermediate term and/or short term depending upon the individual orientation of the trader. In fact, some of the most successful futures traders are "position traders" (i.e., those with an intermediate- to long-term orientation).

Many other misconceptions and misunderstandings plague futures trading, all bred out of either partial information or ignorance. One by one, these myths will be unveiled and corrected as your understanding of futures and futures trading increases. Now that a few of the major myths have been dealt with initially, we can move on to the basics of futures trading.

WHAT IS A "FUTURE"?

The best way to describe a futures contract is by example. I will assume that you have no understanding of the futures market.

Suppose you are a grain farmer. You grow corn. Your crop has been planted and the summer suddenly becomes hot and dry. Rain is scarce in most parts of the country and some of the large grain-processing firms become concerned about what will happen to corn prices several months in the future as the heat and drought damage take their toll of the crop. In your area however, weather is not as bad and moisture has been sufficient. Your crops are quite good, in fact.

The grain-processing concerns such as large baking companies, animal feed manufacturers, food processors, vegetable oil producers, and other related concerns begin to buy corn from farmers and grain firms who have it in storage from previous years. Their buying is considerable due to their immense needs. Simple economics tells us that the price of corn will rise as the supply falls.

Prices begin to rise dramatically. In what is called the "cash market." (This is the immediate or day-to-day market.) Another term for the cash market is the "spot market." It is so termed because it refers to transactions made on the spot, that is for immediate delivery, not for delivery at some point in the future.

Assume that you know the cost of production for your corn. In other words, you've taken into consideration your fertilizer, fuel, land, labor and additional costs. You conclude that it costs you $1.85 to produce each bushel of corn. Your call to the local grain terminal where cash corn is bought and sold tells you that today cash corn is selling for $3.25 per bushel. Only two weeks ago it was at $3 per bushel and three months ago it was at $2.75. You know that you will be producing over 50,000 bushels of corn this year and, as a consequence, the price difference between what the market was several months ago and today's price is considerable. In fact, it runs into thousands of dollars.

What are your options? You know that by the time your crop has been harvested, prices may be back down again. What could force prices back down? Many things could happen. The government could release grain from its reserves to drive prices down, foreign production could be larger than expected making the U.S. crop reduction less important, or weather could improve significantly lessening the impact of the problem. Demand could decline and the grain companies might sell from some of the supplies they've accumulated.

Regardless of what actually happens, you've decided that you want to sell your crop at the current price. You can do either of two things:

1. You can enter into a forward contract with a grain firm. This contract is made between yourself and a grain processor or elevator (these firms are known as "commercials"). They will quote you a price for your crop to be delivered to them at some point in the future, usually shortly after harvest. Often their price is not as high as what the market is currently trading at.
2. As an alternative, you could sell your crop on the futures market. The futures markets are organized exchanges or marketplaces where many individuals congregate for the purpose of buying and selling contracts in given markets for future delivery and/or for speculation. Prices there will be relatively free of manipulation by large commercial interests, which may have almost complete control over what you will be paid in your home-town area for your crop.

Provided your corn meets the proper exchange specifications you can sell it in advance on the futures exchange. You will not get your money until the crop is delivered to the buyer, but, the price you get will be locked in. Regardless of where the price goes thereafter, you will be guaranteed the price at which you sold your crop.

You could win or lose. If the cash market is higher by the time the crop is ready, you will not make as much as you might have. If the price is lower, then you are fortunate in having sold prior to the decline. Of course, you have the option of doing nothing, hoping that prices will be much higher at some point in the future.

The essence of the futures market vehicle is, therefore, in its use as a tool by which the producer and end-user can "hedge" or protect profits. Futures are ideal hedges against rising or falling prices.

WHAT'S IN IT FOR THE "PLAYERS"?

Who takes the other side of the futures transaction and why? In other words, who will buy the grain from you, why will they buy it, what will they do with it, and how will they sell it if they change their mind? Essentially, there are three categories of "players" in the futures game. They are as follows:

Producers

These individuals and/or firms actually produce or process the commodity that is being traded. Whether it be silver, gold, petroleum, corn, live cattle, lumber, sugar or currencies, these are the people who make the goods available either by growing them, harvesting them, mining them, lending them, etc. They need to lock in costs. In other words, they have a product they want to sell at a determined price. They may do this in order to guarantee a profit on an actual commodity item they have on hand or have produced, or they may want to lock in a price on an item in order to avoid losing more money on it if it is already declining.

Finally, they may not have the goods at all, rather they may be protecting themselves from a possible side effect of declining or rising prices. For example, a jewelry store with considerable gold and silver jewelry on hand may fear a decline in the price of precious metals. They stand to lose money on their inventory as prices decline. Therefore, they may choose to sell futures contracts of silver and/or gold in expectation of the decline. Thus, they have profited from the futures sale.

End-Users

These are the people who will use the stuff that's sold by producers. They need to lock in the cost of their production by advance purchase of raw goods. Therefore, they will buy either on the futures market or they may make a forward contract (previously defined).

At times the end-user may become a seller as opposed to a buyer. Assume, for example, that too much has been purchased or that the final product is not selling well. In such an event, the end-user may switch to the sell side.

The producer may at times switch sides, as well. Assume that the firm does not have enough production to meet obligations to others. The producer may then become a buyer as opposed to a seller. As you can see, roles in futures trading can change.

Speculators

This is the largest group of futures traders. These people are sandwiched between the end-user and the producer, providing a market buffer. Perhaps no more than 1 to 3 percent of all futures contracts are actually completed by delivery. The balance are closed out before any actual exchange of goods occurs.

Suffice it to say that speculators are often willing to take risk in markets at times and at prices that may not be attractive to the other two groups. Speculators do this in expectation of large percentage profit returns on price fluctuations. The following table shows the general relationship between the three basic groups of market participants. More details will be given as your understanding of basic concepts increases.

TABLE 1
PLAYERS IN THE FUTURES MARKETS AND THEIR USUAL ROLES

Producers	*Speculators*	*End-Users*
Sell to lock in profits. Can buy at times. Are usually farmers, banks, mining firms, manufacturers, etc. Often called "hedgers."	Buy or sell to make a profit, but not to use the actual goods or products. Often called "traders" (among other things). Do not take delivery of the goods. Often trade for short-term swings.	Buy in order to use the product in their processing or business concern. Can be sellers at times. May not actually use the goods they buy.

For now I'll spare you many specifics of how futures contracts work. These mechanical things will be learned later. What I want you to learn now are the concepts of futures trading. The basic issue is, of course, why trade? Let's now turn attention to this question.

WHY TRADERS TRADE

At first blush, the answer to this question is obvious. The simple fact of the matter is that traders trade in order to make profits. But there are many aspects to this simple answer. Let's look at a few of the most significant reasons for trading futures.

1. **Futures Trading Requires Relatively Small Start up Capital.**

   Typically, one can get started in futures trading for as little as $10,000. In some cases less capital is required. Many professionally managed trading pools require from $2,500 to $5,000 for participation. While most traders are not successful when starting with limited capital, this is one way to "get your foot in the door."

   Futures options trading requires even less capital.

Therefore, it is possible for the individual to begin with an even smaller amount of capital. In most other areas considerably greater capital is required. The small amount of capital can work for or against you . . . most often against you.

2. **Leverage Is Immense.**

The typical futures contract can be bought or sold for 1 to 3 percent of its total value. For example, a 100 troy ounce gold contract at $400 per ounce ($40,000 cash value) can be bought for about $1,500–$2,000. The balance of the money will, of course, be due if and when the contract is completed (i.e., when you take delivery).

In the meantime, about $2,000 is controlling $40,000. In Treasury bill futures, the contract size is $1 million and the margin is about $2,500. In other words, you have immense profit loss potential using small amounts of money. This can work for you *or* against you. It is the goal of the futures trader to make it work in his or her favor.

3. **Futures Markets Make Big Moves.**

Prices fluctuate dramatically almost every day. There is considerable opportunity to win or lose every day in futures trading. Many markets will permit potential returns of 100 percent or more per day on the required margin money (i.e., money required to buy or sell a contract). This, too, can work for *or* against you. Where there is great opportunity, there is often great risk as well.

4. **Futures Markets Are Very Liquid.**

By this I mean that it is possible to get into or out of a market very quickly. This is not so with many stock and real estate investments. Some speculative stocks rarely trade and real estate is often hard to dispose of quickly. With futures transactions, as with active stock transactions, one can enter and exit within minutes or even seconds. This makes the market ideal for the speculator with limited capital.

5. **There Are Not Many Secrets to Successful Trading.**
   In some areas of investment you need to know either the right people or the right inside information. While correct inside information can be very helpful in trading futures, success does not depend on such information. There are few secrets to successful trading. Good trading is a *skill* that can be learned and that can, in fact, be *taught* very specifically, objectively and successfully to those willing and able to learn.

6. **There Are Many Futures Vehicles.**
   In addition to the traditional buy and sell short positions, there are many vehicles in futures trading. These include options, spreads, option spreads, futures versus options positions, and combinations of the above.

WHAT ABOUT THE RISK?

You've all heard that there is considerable risk in futures trading. There's no denying this fact. The statistics are not in your favor when it comes to the futures markets. As a matter of fact, I've often heard that up to 95 percent of all traders lose their money. How does one get around these statistics?

First and foremost, education is a vital aspect. The trader with a small amount of capital is most apt to lose since he cannot play the game long enough to get into the highly profitable trades. The facts are that the larger your starting amount, the more likely you are to be successful.

In addition, there are many time-tested principles that, if applied with consistency and discipline, will greatly improve the odds in your favor. Statistically, one can be wrong about the market over 50 percent of the time and still make money, provided that losses are limited. *It is the inability to keep losses small that makes most traders losers.*

Furthermore, it is the behavior of taking profits quickly and

losses slowly that can make the statistics work against you. *The
successful trader is quick to limit losses.* I will come back to this
point many times during the course of this book, since it is one
of my goals to teach you the proper *philosophy* of trading, in addition to the *basics of the markets* themselves. I am convinced that
losses can be reduced by a significant degree if one learns how
to limit risk, how to take losses quickly, and how to keep them
small.

Losses are part of every business. In the retail or manufactur-
ing area, for example, losses are comprised of such things as rent,
overhead, insurance, production costs, theft and depreciation. Not
all transactions are profitable. It is, however, the "bottom line" that
differentiates the winners from the losers.

In the final analysis, risk is something each investor and trader
must evaluate in relation to his or her financial situation. It is certain that there is more inherent risk in futures trading as it is commonly practiced today. However, with risk goes reward. Without
risk there cannot be reward of the magnitude common in futures
trading.

ADDITIONAL USES OF THE FUTURES MARKETS

This chapter has, to this point, briefly outlined preliminary
concepts and applications of futures trading. Naturally, as a vehicle for speculating, hedging, or spreading risk, futures trading has
significant importance. As a vehicle for stabilizing costs to
producers and end-users, futures trading is a vital tool.

On a more pervasive level, however, an understanding of
futures trading can prove to be very valuable to the investor not
interested in actually trading futures. This book gives considerable attention to the hypothesis that a knowledge of futures price
trends and futures market behavior can assist one in understanding economic trends as well as in forecasting the short-term to
intermediate-term direction of prices. There may also be long-range
implications for investors.

CONCLUSIONS

Futures trading is a technique whereby one can buy and/or sell a variety of raw and processed commodity items, including financial instruments and stock indices, for anticipated delivery at some point in the future. There are three major categories of participants in the futures markets each with their own expectations, goals and market methods. Futures trading allows producers and end-users to lock in costs of production, improving economic stability as well as the stability of their particular business. Speculators, by far the largest category of traders, have no interest in making or taking delivery, rather, their interest is in playing market swings for dollar profits.

There are many common objections to futures trading. Some have merit; others are not well founded.

There are specific methods, systems and procedures used in futures trading designed to reduce its inherent risk, a majority of which have been time-tested. Futures trading involves considerable risk, however, this risk can be greatly reduced by consistent application of various principles. Futures trading can be an excellent vehicle for immense profit, or it can be a dangerous tool for financial ruin. Who win often attribute their success to self-discipline, consistency, specific trading techniques and persistence.

Part 1

Getting Started:
Myths and Realities
of the Futures Markets

Chapter
1

Dealing with Basic Issues First

It sometimes seems that the older we get, the more complex our lives become. Things which, in our childhood and adolescence, we took for granted as simple and easily understood, we now find more complicated and difficult to explain. Conversely, things which we found, in our childhood, to be the most difficult to understand, we somehow take for granted now as part of our every day lives.

My first exposure to the markets was in an eighth-grade social studies class. The instructor thought it would further our education in economics and the "American Way" "if we were to hypothetically invest a thousand dollars in several stocks we selected from the evening newspaper listings. "Why should we do this?" asked one of the students. "To make our capital grow," replied the teacher.

He expanded upon our assignment by offering the following concise explanation of how the American capitalist system works, (which I have paraphased).

> Our system of economics functions on the basis of supply and demand. Supply and demand make prices go up and down. In order to meet demand, individuals form associations or businesses to supply the goods, services or commodities that the public wishes to consume. However, in order to do this they require capital.

There are many ways in which they can raise the required capital. One of the most common ways is through the issuance of stock. Shares of stock are issued to buyers who will, in effect, lend their money to the company which will, in turn, produce the products, etc. The shareholders reward for lending money to the corporation will be participation in the profits.

Of course, there is no guarantee that profits will be made, and so the purchase of stock is a gesture of good faith and expectation based on the buyer's perception of the company's ability to make good on its business ventures. In addition, if the company does exceptionally well, the demand for its stock will grow and the shareholder can make money in two ways. First, money can be made on a share of profits distributed by the company. Second, money can be made when the stock price goes up in response to demand from individuals wanting to purchase a part (or shares) of that company.

The answer was simple enough and certainly satisfied everyone of us in class. We felt very much like the answer to making money in the stock market was rather simple. Was it Will Rogers who said something like, "Making money in the stock market is simple . . .just find stocks that are going to go up and buy them." The simple-minded solution offered by our teacher was easily accepted by us in those days and, in fact, it was sufficient for many years to come. Now, as I think back to the transition that has occurred both with age and experience, I find that this issue, once elementary, has now become immensely complex.

Similarly, there are many other basic issues, all seemingly simple on the surface, but each highly complex when examined in detail. The balance of this chapter deals with some of these issues, not necessarily in a order of importance, but in considerable detail. These are all issues that each current or prospective speculator must evaluate and assess.

There is always a great temptation for students to skim over the introductory portion of a book in order to get on with the "real meat" of the subject. This book is all "real meat." In fact, I would venture to say that the major substance is contained in the first few chapters as opposed to the last few. So, if you are going to skim, don't skim this chapter!

Take your time. Think each issue through thoroughly and, above all, be honest with yourself. Don't take any of these issues lightly, even though you may be familiar with all of them. The facts of futures trading will not be helpful to you if you do not have a stable backdrop against which to apply them.

GRIST FOR THE MILL

Let's face it, the world of well-dressed brokers, white-collar executives, and the man in the Hathaway shirt who "listens while his broker talks," is not the real world of trading. There is a story behind every trade, and a trade behind every story. More often than not, it is not a very pleasant one.

The tale is not based upon the simple act of picking up a telephone and calling in an order. The true story behind the crisp numbers crossing the ticker tape or flashing on your computer screen is one of competition, psychology, strategy, skill, victory and defeat. The fact of the matter is that a good majority of traders have been and will continue to be losers. Accept this fact now, or you too will be nothing but grist for the mill.

Studies of human behavior clearly show that in order to change behavior, you must acknowledge and recognize its existence. Therefore, if you think that the key to successful trading is simply to acquire more information, then it is time to rethink your thinking.

In order to avoid the unfortunate fate of most speculators, you will need to think and act in a fashion contrary to most traders. You will use the available market tools, but you will reach different conclusions and you will take different actions. In order to do this you will need to:

1. Examine your objectives and recognize the problems (if any),
2. Formulate your plan of action and solve the problems,
3. Make a commitment,
4. Select the vehicle you will use to transport you to your goals.
5. Put your plans into action with consistency and discipline.

Knowledge alone cannot be the key to effective action. The gap between knowledge and action is one of the most vast expanses known to humankind. This is the ultimate frontier of inner space.

In order to make money in futures trading, you will have to find a way to legally take money from other traders before they take it from you. In futures trading the cold hard facts are simply these: For every winner there is a loser; for every dollar made, there is a dollar lost; you can profit only at the expense of someone else's loss. If you don't make others the grist for your mill, you will become the grist for theirs (unless you decide not to play the game).

EXAMINING OUR OBJECTIVES

None of us, including this writer, will ever attain the level of perfection we truly seek to achieve in futures trading. The first lesson in establishing objectives is to keep your goals realistic. There are some definite yardsticks against which we can judge our expectations. In reality, we may secretly wish and hope to surpass these yardsticks by a significant amount, but we should not overestimate our abilities by placing our expectations beyond the realm of the real futures world.

What, then, is "realistic"? Let's examine the facts in terms of performance and profits. First let's take a look at the performance of professionally managed funds over an extended period of time. Managed Account Reports[1] states that, of the professionally managed commodity funds now in operation, one of the largest cumulative percentage profits since inception amounted to 30.4 percent. This covered a period of six years. Note that since commodity managed funds began reporting their results, approximately 14.5 percent of them have been liquidated at losses of 50 percent or greater.

The best overall performance of such programs is in the area of 19.1–30.4 percent of starting equity. Remember, this is not taking into consideration the funds that have been closed out at 50 percent losses or more.[2]

[1]Lee Rose. *Managed Accounts Reports.* 5513 Twin Knolls Road, Suite 213, Columbia, Maryland, 21045.

[2]Figures through end of 1985.

In order to have realistic expectations, we can use the foregoing parameters of performance as our guidelines. Taking an average, you can see that 19–31 percent profits per year is a realistic expectation. Don't be dismayed—19–31 percent compounded at an annual rate works out to be a very high figure.

CAN YOU MAKE THE COMMITMENT?

Consider the results I have just discussed. These results were obtained by full-time professionals in the commodity business. Their work required a major commitment of time and effort. Although it is probably true that there is not a one-to-one relationship between profits and efforts extended in the futures markets, it is true that considerable effort is necessary in order to achieve reasonably good results.

Although one may have an intense desire to make profits in futures trading, achievement does not necessarily follow directly from desire. The intervening variable is work. You must assess your efforts and goals realistically in terms of the time commitment you can make.

The world is long on ambition, but short on effort. But effort, in and of itself, is not necessarily synonymous with profit. Effort must be directed at a particular goal. It must be guided through proper steps. Effort must be aimed in the right direction. Effort must be self-correcting. Mistakes must be used for learning. All of this takes time! Perhaps the greatest favor you can do for yourself is to be realistic in terms of time. This leads to the next issue.

HOW WILL YOU ACHIEVE YOUR GOAL?

There are many ways to get to your goal. The goal of profits in futures trading can be achieved through long-term trading, short-term trading, speculating on an intraday basis, spreading, options trading, option spreads, floor trading, as a broker, or by a combination of these strategies. In addition, there are many vehicles which can lead you toward, or away from, your goals.

You must make some important decisions. You must decide how you will achieve your goals. Some of these decisions can be made based on your present state of knowledge. Others, however, cannot be made until you have expanded your knowledge and understanding of the field. I would suggest that even if you feel you have already know the answers to these issues, you come back and reread this section after you have finished reading the entire book. In future chapters, I will rekindle some of these burning issues, providing you with some suggestions as to their resolution.

THE VEHICLE

Many vehicles can take you to your goal. Some are ideally suited to your direction, whereas others will take you in the wrong direction. These vehicles are the systems and methods of futures trading.

I can't tell you which system is best for you. All I can do is to acquaint you with the various methods and with guidelines for deciding which techniques are best for you. The performance of trading systems is not static. Systems go through good times as well as bad. Traders go through good times as well as bad. Traders and systems interact in a complex combination.

I *can't* give you the ultimate answers, but I *can* acquaint you with the tools. I can give you the knowledge to help you make your own decisions based upon the facts. As you read the remainder of this book, keep your mind tuned to the issues I have just raised, looking for answers as you go. Assuming that you have already had some experience in this area, you will recognize the answers more easily.

THE FUEL

In your travels you will need a goal, a vehicle, and fuel. We have already discussed the vehicle and the goal. Now we must look at the fuel.

The energy that drives the wheel of successful speculation is good old-fashioned money. To make it, you have to have it, and to multiply it you have to use it wisely. You know that risk is immense and that the odds are stacked against you. Your chances of making it in the competitive world of futures trading are probably 5 or 10 in 100, but, you can't make it by starting with nothing. Successful speculation is not a get-rich-quick scheme, a "no money down" real estate venture or a 15 million-to-one odds lottery ticket. The facts of futures trading life dictate very clearly that the more you start with, the greater the chance of success, and the less you start with, the greater your chance of failure.

"How much is enough?" you ask. I can give you some guidelines. Based on 1986 conditions in the futures market the beginner should have sufficient capital to meet liberal marginal requirements on at least five contracts in the futures market. If we assume, for example, that the average margin on a futures contract is $2,500, then we are looking at approximately $12,500 in speculative capital. I don't think it is realistic for you to expect success if you begin with less.

Don't be fooled! Some individuals will tell you that you need virtually nothing in the way of starting capital, whereas others will tell you you need much, much more. I won't argue the fact that the more you have to start with the better your odds of success; however, there is a limit on the downside. Certainly you must consider the fact that you don't want to risk everything.

When someone asks me how much they should risk in futures trading I answer the question with a question. I ask, "How much can you afford to lose?" One answer might be "$10,000." "Take this slip of paper on which I have written $10,000," I respond, "rip it into shreds. Flush it down the toilet. How do you feel?"

This small test represents a little experiment that may help you determine how much you can afford to lose in the futures market without too serious an emotional reaction to the consequences. Financially, the answer is different. How much can you afford to lose from this standpoint? I would suggest that as a rule of thumb, you risk not more than 25 percent of your total, liquid, risk capital!

DON'T BORROW YOUR STARTING CAPITAL

Let me caution you against a practice I have witnessed on a number of occasions during my years in the futures market. It has become more and more common for individuals to borrow money in order to speculate in futures. Specifically, second mortgages or home equity loans are often used for this purpose. I recommend that this foolhardy behavior be entirely avoided. There is no sound judgment in such behavior and the results of such actions are more often than not very unfavorable. The individual not only places him- or herself at financial risk, but jeopardizes his or her trading by using funds that should not and cannot be placed at risk. Certainly it takes no great insight to see that this will seriously affect the judgment and trading decisions of the speculator.

Another pitfall to avoid is the following intellectualization or rationalization! "I'll put more money into my account than I intend to lose, but the rest will draw interest and, of course, I will watch the money closely." As I explained, this is a rationalization, and certainly not a productive one at that! *Put into your account only that which you can afford to lose in its entirety.*

Don't be fooled by the lure of interest rate earnings on the unused funds, especially low-risk trading programs, failsafe programs, "no risk" option strategies, minimal risk spreading programs, and a host of other seemingly simple, "minimal risk" programs. I've seen them come and I've seen them go. There are some big winners, but there are many, many more big losers. Do not accept the claims of any trading system, your own or that of someone else, as the basis for deciding how much of your money you will place at risk.

REACH YOUR GOAL BY STAGES

Even in today's age of space travel and instant communications, it is still necessary to reach one's destination in stages or steps

Unfortunately, or perhaps fortunately, our dimension in time and space does not permit thoughts to become actions and, therefore, goals must be attained slowly. Whether you decide to trade for the short term, intermediate term, or long term, it is advisable that you regularly withdraw profits from your account once you have reached a certain level of successful performance. Generally, I recommend 10 to 25 percent of profits from each and every winning trade be removed from your account. This need not be done on a trade by trade basis. You can do it weekly or perhaps bi-monthly, but remember to do it!

More speculators would be successful if they approached futures trading from the standpoint of a business. After a period of learning and initial cost, a business that reaches the point of profitable operation will generate income for its operator(s). The profits are then taken and employed in some other fashion not directly connected with the business itself. Some of the other profits are turned back into the business in order to expand its base.

It is the same with futures trading. On occasion, speculators have achieved tremendous initial growth in their accounts. Lured by greed and the promise of even greater profits, they have plowed every penny, if not more, back into the market only to lose it all. When all is said and done, they had nothing to show for their great efforts.

This is why you must formulate and institute a specific program for systematically removing a percentage of your profits from your trading account. This rule is applicable whether you are speculating for the long term, short term or in between terms.

OTHER IMPORTANT ISSUES

In addition to the points just raised, a number of important issues warrant attention by all aspiring futures traders, regardless of their eventual orientation, system or trading methodology. I will review some of these briefly at this time, covering them in greater detail as the occasions present themselves in future chapters.

1. **Trade Alone or with a Partner?**

   There are pros and cons to each alternative. If you trade alone, there will be no one to help you with your work (unless you hire employees) and there will be no one that can trade for you in your absence. Furthermore, there will be no one with whom you can discuss various markets, indicators, techniques and trades. To those individuals who need this type of assistance, a partner or well-trained assistant might be desirable. However, before you make such a decision consider the potential negatives of having a partner.

   a. **Too Many Cooks Spoil the Pie.** Futures tradings is a "loner's game." Sometimes a partner or partners will get in your way, both literally and figuratively. You may be influenced to avoid some trades you should have made and to make some trades you should have avoided.

   b. **Who's Responsible?** In developing your trading, it is always good to know that you alone have the responsibility for profits and losses. If you have a partner or partners, it may be difficult to know who is responsible for each decision. Lacking such knowledge will slow the learning process and may, in fact, stall it entirely.

   c. **Sharing the Profits.** Do you really want to share your profits with partners? Granted, they may also share in your losses, but since you may end up with more losses if you have partners, the benefits may prove nil.

   d. **Do You Want to Share Your Research?** Many of us consider our research proprietary. We work long, hard hours to develop trading systems and methods and we may not want to share these with a partner regardless what he or she may bring into the relationship.

   e. **Slower Decision Time.** As you know, decisions in the futures markets must be made quickly. Many times the presence of a trading partner may slow down the making process and, hence, severely limit the speed with which you can execute orders. This, as you can well imagine, can frequently have negative results.

2. **Trade for the Short Term, Long Term or in Between?**
   I could write several books just addressing this subject.
   There are so many variables to consider, not the least important of which are your personality and temperament. Here
   are just a few of the factors you should consider in making
   this decision.

   a. **Trading System.** Some trading systems are more
      ideally suited to short-term trading, while others are bet-
      ter suited to long-term trading.

   b. **Time Availability.** Only you know how much time you
      have available. To trade for the short term or intraday
      you will need to make a major time commitment. If you
      have another job and you can't make this commitment,
      don't even try! Be realistic and determine what you can
      do with the time you have available. This may automat-
      ically make your decision for you without further
      consideration.

   c. **Commissions.** Are you paying sufficiently low com-
      missions to permit short-term trading with a positive bot-
      tom line?

   d. **Personality.** Can you take the pressure of short-term
      trading? Are you more in tune with long-term trading
      and its less demanding pace?

   e. **Health.** Believe it or not, health is a consideration. If
      your health is at stake, then by all means don't push your
      luck. Trade with that period of time or that length of time
      which will best be suited to these needs. Answering this
      question honestly will help make many decisions for you
      without considering any of the other aspects.

   f. **Data.** Many individuals are under the false impression
      that they can day-trade the market without a steady
      source of tick-by-tick data. Don't fool yourself! To day-
      trade you need up to date, tick-by-tick, accurate and relia-
      ble data. If you can't afford it, if you don't know how to
      use it, then don't kid yourself. Day trading is not for you.
      In addition to the above there are other factors which

are specific to your individual situation that must be considered before a final decision is made about the type of trading you wish to do. This is an important decision. Do not take it lightly.

3. **Fundamentals or Technicals**

Another important decision which should ideally be made prior to the start of your trading is whether your approach will focus primarily upon trading signals from technical indicators or from trading ideas based upon fundamentals. I distinguish here between "ideas" and "signals" because they are two distinctly different types of approaches generated by two distinctly different understandings of the futures markets.

Later on I will provide a very thorough discussion of the two approaches, outlining their strengths, assets, liabilities, differences and methods of implementation. For now, suffice it to say that a decision will need to be made, preferably sooner than later, about the approach you wish to employ in your trading. Some individuals may seek to implement a hybrid approach, incorporating what they feel are the best aspects of each technique. I will also discuss the merits of this approach, or the lack thereof.

4. **How Much Risk Do You Want to Take on Each Trade?**

A significant question, one that is perhaps best answered prior to the start of trading is, "How much do you want to risk on each trade?" Many factors enter into this decision. There are certainly many different opinions regarding the best answer.

On opposite ends of the continuum, we find the two extreme approaches. Those who belong to the "money management school" will tell you that the best approach to take is a per-trade risk based strictly on money management. In other words, you decide ahead the maximum risk you want to take, in dollars. When a trade goes against you by the predetermined amount, you close it out.

On the other end of the continuum is the "systems approach." Proponents of this approach claim that each trade is unique. Every trade has specific levels of support and resistance and, therefore, it is not possible to determine *a priori* a rule for dollar risk. My approach to this aspect in futures trading is essentially similar to my approach in other areas. I prefer not to be in the middle of the road. Rather, I would align myself with either of the extremes.

As you continue to read this book, you will understand more clearly why my preference is usually to be found on one end of the spectrum, or the other, but rarely in the middle. It's been said that "you can walk on the left side of the road or the right side of the road, but if you walk in the middle of the road you will get squashed."

There are merits to each approach and there is no right or wrong answer to the question. There is, however, an answer that is your answer. My job is to help you find it. Hopefully, buy the time you have finished this book, you will have found the answer falling naturally into place. For the time being, however, I will tell you that each approach has its strong and weak points and you can be successful by following each of the extremes.

SELECTING A BROKER

This topic is so important that I have devoted a full chapter to it. You needn't make the decision now. Many of you may, in fact, already have a broker (or brokers).

A broker can help you or hurt you. I do not contend that brokers intentionally hurt customers. Certainly this would not be in their best interest. I am saying, however, that on various levels, the relationship between broker and client is extremely important. I maintain that insufficient attention has been given to this variable. Virtually no book I've read on successful methods of speculation places sufficient emphasis on this variable and its potentially positive/negative implications. When you are done reading this book, your ideas about the broker/client relationship will likely have changed significantly.

The foregoing issues are ones that you should consider prior to serious speculation in the futures markets. There will be many other important issues raised by this book, but, the ones outlined in this chapter should incubate within your unconscious mind while you read the chapters that follow.

I want to stress that some of the material discussed in the balance of this book will not be new to you. In fact, I am certain that the issues I have discussed in this chapter are ones with which you are essentially familiar with right now. Don't let the "oldness" of the ideas stand in the way of your acquiring new and valuable understandings of old information. If you consider the fact that most market analysts and speculators have the same information at their disposal, but that some use it with considerably more success than others, you will understand that the difference between losers and winners is not necessarily that winners have better tools, but rather that they use their tools better. How to use tools for maximum results is what this book will attempt to teach you.

SUMMARY

Success in the futures markets can come only at the expense of other traders' failures. The factors affecting success were identified and discussed. Guidelines were set out for realistic objectives in light of performance and committed effort was stressed. Amount and sources of starting capital needed were discussed, along with a procedure for withdrawing proceeds from profitable trades. The benefits and drawbacks of trading with a partner were covered. Long-, short- and intermediate-term time orientations were considered, as were preferences for technical or fundamental trading systems and the choice among levels of risk. The broker-client relationship was discussed briefly.

Chapter

2

Trading Approaches: Fundamental Versus Technical Analysis

Let's begin by plunging head-first into a basic controversy. Since this book will ultimately ruffle the feathers of many concepts and beliefs revered by a majority of speculators, let's not waste any time before the iconoclasm begins. Let's look at what I call the "good, the bad and the ugly." I am, of course, jokingly referring to fundamentals, technicals and the peculiar offspring of their marriage, that one might, for public relations purposes, term "eclectics."

We'll take a little critical overview of the two major approaches, then we'll examine their hybrid in order to see which, if any, might be the most desirable approach. Please understand that what is being expressed herein are the opinions of one speculator. They may be right, they may be wrong. They may ultimately be proven valid or invalid, but, they are designed to stimulate thought, and in so doing, to promote positive change. The markets function on the basis of opinion. We all know that opinions are plentiful. However, opinions based on considerable experience are neither dismissed lightly, nor available freely.

FUNDAMENTAL ANALYSIS

What in heaven's name is a fundamental? I have often asked myself this question. It seems that everything is fundamental. Do we mean fundamental as opposed to trivial; or fundamental in the sense of basic; or fundamental in the sense of building block? Let's look at a recent definition of the term as found in the *Handbook of Futures Markets.*[1] Note also some of the points raised by the analysis:

The fundamentalist uses historical economic information to establish a supply-and-demand price curve. He or she then relates estimates of this year's supply-and-demand balance to the historical price to decide if the current price is too high, too low, or just right. To arrive at an estimate of this year's supply, the fundamentalist will examine reports of the number of acres planted on a particular crop. The fundamentalist will also look at the sales of fertilizer and the sales and cost of diesel fuel for farm equipment, in addition to past weather data and predicted weather patterns for both the near- and longer-term periods of the crop's growing season. Information must be taken into account about the productivity of new seeds or strains developed for the crop being considered or for competing crops. The fundamentalist must be aware of the government stockpiles as well as those stockpiled on-farm (visible supply). Government price-support levels and the strength of the dollar will be considered, as it affects exports. The analyst will weigh the cost of interest paid on borrowed money, the impact of competition from substitutes or new products, and will be alert to changes in eating patterns and per capita income affecting demand. This list would have to be extended significantly to include all the primary determinants of price, and yet the accuracy of the current price evaluation depends upon the accuracy of the estimates and the weighting of factors. Do not be convinced that because of the complexity of the information involved, no fundamental method, as we have defined it, can be possible. There are econometric formulas which can reduce this mass of data to

[1]P.J. Kaufman (Wiley: New York, 1985), 16.5.

specific values, using computers, with respect to the current price and provide adequate information for trading purposes.

The difficulty with the fundamental approach for most speculators is that vast amounts of time and money can be consumed to obtain the past and present data and to work it into reliable formulations. To continue to update this data each day would then be the task of a full-time staff. (Time-sharing computer services which provide this information are equally expensive.) The individual trader who wishes to use the fundamental approach is in direct competition with the largest producers and processors in the world, with their relatively unlimited resources of information and analysis. In such a competition, the outcome is not often a surprise.

Fundamentals, then are the stuff, or the economic realities, that ultimately affect price. Fundamentalists, then, are those who somehow formulate a trading plan or trading approach on the basis of fundamentals. In other words, they take the basics of supply/demand, and determine whether prices should increase or decrease. On the basis of these *expectations*, they make buy and sell decisions.

Fundamental analysis has its roots in economics. Economic theory is not just one theory, rather there are many economic theories. Similarly, there are many different approaches to fundamental analysis. The common element of all approaches to fundamental analysis is that they study the purported causes of price increases and price decreases in the hope that they will be able to ascertain changes prior to their occurrences. Their success rests upon the availability of accurate assessments of the variables they analyze, as well as the availability of variables that may not be known to other fundamental analysts.

The plethora of statistics available to the fundamentalist at any given point in time can be overwhelming. The fundamentalist must be selective, and prepared to evaluate a massive amount of data.

There is no one typical fundamentalist. We won't find a cage in the zoo labelled, "Analyticus Fundamentalis." Rather, there are many different types of fundamentalists, who evaluate different types of data at different times. There are those who, by virtue of their skill and their expertise, can provide accurate forecasts, and there are those who, working the same tools, make worthless forecasts.

SHORTCOMINGS OF FUNDAMENTAL ANALYSIS

The age and cost of computer technology has, unfortunately, overshadowed the excellent work being done by many individual researchers in the area of fundamental analysis. The tendency of modern society to look for quick and easy solutions to problems has been partially responsible for the shift away from public implementation of fundamental analysis. On the other hand, however, the contemporary trend toward more simple solutions has in part, been stimulated by the difficulty and complexity of fundamental analysis.

The average individual will have very limited success in understanding, analyzing and implementing massive amounts of fundamental statistics. Even if all relevant statistics were available, the average individual would have difficulty interpreting their meaning as it relates to the important issue of futures trading, which is *timing*. Some of the difficulties with fundamental analysis can be summarized as follows:

1. Not all fundamentals can be known at any given point in time.
2. The importance of different fundamentals varies at different times. It is difficult to know which fundamentals are most significant at which time.
3. The average speculator may have difficulty gathering and interpreting the wealth of information that is available for every market.
4. Fundamental analysis often fails to answer the important question that faces most speculators, the question of timing.
5. Most fundamental statistics are available after the fact. By the time they are gathered by various government agencies or reporting services throughout the world, they are often old information and do not necessarily reflect the immediate situation.
6. Fundamentals can be significantly altered by abrupt changes such

as weather, politics, international events and some technical factors. It may take time for these items to be reflected in the actual fundamental statistics.

7. The amount of effort required in gathering, updating and interpreting fundamental data may not, in the long run, yield efficient dividends in terms of results.

8. Most fundamental analysis does not provide alternatives based on price action, but rather it provides alternatives based on changes in underlying conditions. These changes may be so slow that no visible or perceptible alterations in bullish or bearish stance might be justified when, in fact, a major change in trend may have begun.

Yet, in spite of these shortcomings, fundamental analysis still has its place in the commodity world. Ultimately, the price of every commodity is a function of fundamentals. Unfortunately, fundamental analysis has been the whipping boy of market technicians for many years now. Whether justified or not, this has led to an understatement of its importance.

Rest assured that the fundamentals are very important and that their implementation can yield significant results *over the long term.* I maintain that fundamental analysis has its place for the intermediate- and long-term trader. However, for the short-term speculator I would suggest that fundamentals are not likely to yield the results you seek. The individual who is willing to establish a major position, stick with the position, give it plenty of leeway, and possibly add to the position on a scale-in basis, can do very well. This is the proper place for the fundamentalist.

Typically, individuals employed to provide price forecasts, hedging patterns, purchasing programs, and planning programs for commercial end-users or suppliers are especially good at understanding and implementing fundamentals. These individuals are not primarily concerned with timing. Frequently they can ride through virtually any storm. The speculator however, cannot use the same approach since his or her capital, time, patience and tolerance are limited by the constraint of available resources.

SUMMARY

Fundamental analysis is not the anathema so many contemporary traders consider it to be. Fundamentals form the basis of the economic equation. Too often they will be proven correct, after the fact with virtually 100 percent accuracy. Even such unexpected events as changes in weather will ultimately be reflected in the fundamental statistics, forecasting price level and direction, but response time can be slow.

The interpretation of fundamentals is both a science and an art which most speculators and average futures traders will have difficulty implementing. Experience and knowledge are especially important in the analysis and implementation of fundamentals. They cannot be acquired as quickly as can the experience in the area of technical analysis.

If you are still interested in the application of fundamentals, I suggest that you take the following advice to heart:

1. Study economics and economic theories thoroughly. Acquaint yourself with the various micro and macro economic theories, particularly as they apply to production and consumption.
2. Acquire a thorough knowledge about the production, consumption, critical factors and implementation of the various commodities that you wish to trade.
3. Attempt to specialize, but do not exclude all other markets from your perspective. There are so many factors to consider that you cannot keep abreast of many markets and economic trends. You cannot be in touch with all market factors and all markets at one time, even with the aid of a computer. Therefore, you ought to specialize in one or two groups of markets (i.e., meats, grains, metals, currencies, etc.)
4. Plan to spend several years learning the application of fundamentals. This is a highly complex field, one which is not mastered easily. Once mastered, however, the benefits can be substantial for the intermediate- and long-term trader (investor).

TECHNICAL SYSTEMS

With the exception of a complete novice to futures trading, virtually everyone is familiar with one or several aspects of technical analysis. Technical analysis is loosely defined as a study of futures trading data and its derivatives with the goal of forecasting price and/or determining specific market timing. In plain old English, this means that the technical analyst studies such things as price, volume, open interest, and chart patterns, as well as the interrelations, permutations and combinations on this theme. The goal of most technical analysis is not necessarily prediction, it is the determination of specific entry and exit levels, and/or specific price objectives for each signal. But prediction is not a requirement. Entry and exit signals alone are quite sufficient.

The roots of technical analysis dig deeply into the history of futures trading. It is difficult to say with certainty who the first individual or group to employ technical analysis might have been. I am certain, however, that traces of technical analysis can probably be found as far back as ancient civilizations. Since technical analysis prides itself on having a quasi-scientific basis, you can understand that the continued exponential growth of scientific methodology has spilled over into the area of technical analysis (as well as fundamental analysis). As a consequence there are literally hundreds of systems, methods, techniques, and trading approaches based on technical concepts.

Technical analysis certainly has its place in the world of futures trading, but as you might have guessed it certainly has its limitations, as well. It is my conclusion that technical analysis is more suitable for short-term trading than for long-term trading. Although there are certain technical methods which may be applied to long-term charts the intricacies of technical analysis do not easily lend themselves to such things as contract changes (i.e., length of contract life) in the futures market.

Specifically, long-term technical analysis must employ long-term data. The only continuous long term data available to futures analysts is cash market data. Futures data starts and stops with contract expirations and contract inceptions. The variability of prices from one contract to another as a function of such things as carrying charges, storage charges and interest rates creates a gap that must be filled either by creation of artificial data or by some other statistical manipulation that is not necessarily representative of true underlying conditions. Due to this fact, there have been a number of different approaches to technical analysis on weekly and monthly charts, resulting in some disagreement among followers of the various techniques.

Some of the criticisms of technical analysis are as follows:

1. Pure technical analysis ignores all extraneous inputs such as news, fundamentals, weather, etc. This is seen as a detriment by some, since these factors can and do significantly affect prices.
2. Technical analysis is a form of tunnel vision, since it accepts input from no other method or technique when employed in its ideal form.
3. Technical analysis is so widely used, particularly by computer-generated trading programs, that many systems act in unison, thereby affecting prices in a fashion that is not representative of the true price structures.
4. Technical analysis cannot allow for good forecasting or determination of price objectives since it does not account for underlying economic conditions.
5. Technical analysis is not a valid scientific approach since most methods of technical analysis analyze prices based upon price-related data. In a sense, one is attempting to predict the outcome of a dependent variable based upon the history of the dependent variable. If the variable is indeed dependent upon circumstances external to it, then it is a fallacy to attempt such predictions without knowing the external circumstances.
6. Technical analysis is a self-fulfilling prophecy and clearly typifies the greater fool theory.[2] In the end, it is the individual who is stuck with the "hot potato" who pays the price of being the greatest fool.

These, then, are some of the objections to technical analysis. On the positive side, however, technical analysis attains its strength from the fact that it is a form of disciplined and essentially mechanical application of trading rules. In its ideal form, technical analysis

[2]For those who are not familiar with the greater fool theory, it is the belief that if one buys a particular stock, commodity or piece of property, one need only wait for someone else who is a greater fool to sell it to.

leaves little or no room for interpretations of trading signals. In this way, it permits discipline to regulate trading. Naturally, these are all ideal concepts and their application is most certainly dependent upon the individual. Some advantages of the purely technical approach are:

1. **Objectivity:**   The technical approach, in ideal form, is objective and specific. It is akin to scientific methodology.
2. **Specificity:**   The technical approach looks for specific indications from the data and then acts upon them. Hence, there should be little or no room for interpretation in a purely technical method.
3. **Mechanical:**   Many technical analysts claim that their approach is totally mechanical. In other words, no thought must go into the buying/selling decisions. The system makes all of the judgments and the trader follows them mechanically (when the system is implemented in its ideal form).
4. **Testable:**   All results and indicators can be tested and verified historically. This makes the approach more scientific and lends credence to its use and value.
5. **Cross-User Reliability:**   The technical approach should yield similar results regardless of who is using the system, provided their rules are the same. Ideally this is *not* the case with many technical approaches, since they leave a certain amount of room for interpretation.
6. **Ease of Application:**   By virtue of the above, technical systems are claimed to be easier to implement than are fundamentally based systems.
7. **Computer Application:**   Recently, the advent of lower-priced personal computer systems has made technical systems even less difficult to test and employ. Most truly mechanical systems can be programmed into computers, which will generate all buy and sell signals accurately. In some cases computers can even be programmed to send the signals to a broker for execution.

There is much to be said in favor of technical analysis. However, with the growing ability of computer systems to work with complex econometric models, I expect to see fundamentally based computer models reach a growing level of impact on futures trading during the late 1980s. The result could very well be a hybrid approach that yields better performance than each method alone. This, however, is not yet the case. Whether technical, fundamental or techofundamental, the ultimate action taken by the speculator will determine the success or failure of any trading system, regardless of how promising computer tests of the system may be.

WHAT'S BEST FOR YOU

It is my observation that individuals who adhere strictly to one approach or another can do well in the marketplace. However, individuals who are constantly shifting from one technical approach to another, from one fundamental approach to another or from an essentially fundamental point of view to a technical point of view will probably not do well. This is because they do not allow sufficient time for their trading approach to reach fruition.

The answer to the question, "What's best for you?" is not a simple one. After years of analysis and study, I can tell you that virtually any systematic approach to futures trading can be successful, provided that it contains three essential elements. These are as follows:

1. **Specific Entry and Exit Indicators.** By this I mean that rules for entering and exiting trades must be as specific and mechanical as possible. Interpretation and deliberations about the validity of a given indicator must be kept to an absolute minimum. There should also be reliability between different users of the method. In other words, two individuals using the same approach on the same market at different locations and without collaboration should ideally reach the same conclusion.
2. **Money Management.** In order for a system to be successful it must have an automatic way to limit losses. There should be a maximum permissible dollar loss or a specific level beyond which losses should not go on, regardless of what the system says.

3. **Flexibility.** The system must be sufficiently flexible to trade both sides of the market, long and short. Furthermore, the system should do well in all types of markets, trending and trendless (though this is a lot to ask for).

SUCCESS AT THE EXTREMES

Provided these essential elements are present, and provided the method of selection has a slightly greater probability than chance, the end result should be profitable. Many systems are capable of generating trading signals that are profitable more than 50 percent of the time. Many approaches, both technical and fundamental, could have even better performance by applying various trend filters.

For now, suffice it to say that the technical approach to money management can yield excellent results. The same is true of the fundamental approach. However, the middle road—technical and fundamental, or a variety of a different technical systems all applied at one time, or a variety of different fundamental techniques all applied at one time—is likely to produce poor results.

As you read on and attempt to find answers best suited to your needs, take into consideration the points I have raised in this chapter and do not make your decisions quickly. Finally, consider the possibility that no specific system may be necessary in order for your results to be profitable. Successful traders are found at both ends of the continuum.

SUMMARY

The choice to follow fundamentals or technicals is a difficult one but, it is one that must be made on the basis of existing realities. While there has been much negative comment in recent years about the value of fundamentals, the fact remains that fundamentals are the ultimate factors that determine price. For the average speculator, however, the time, cost and competition with large firms make fundamental analysis a difficult prospect. Technical trading approaches will work well, provided they are applied in a thorough and disciplined fashion. They are less costly, less time consuming and more adaptable to today's computer technology. Hence, they are the method of choice for most speculators.

Chapter

3

What You Need to Know about Trendlines

One of the most popular techniques of chart analysis is the use of trendlines or establishing levels of support, and resistance, and buy and sell signals. The method is "as old as the hills," and has, at some time in some way, been studied by virtually every futures trader.

Trendlines appear to have validity, yet most traders are unfamiliar with a number of important aspects of trendline analysis. First, let's take a look at the definition of trendline analysis. The definition is important in order to keep our methods and procedures as operational as possible. This, in turn, reduces inconsistency and with it the degree of error.

My definition of a trendline is *a line connecting a minimum of three nonconsecutive turning points on a chart.* You can certainly see that a definition of this nature is so general as to leave considerable room for interpretation (as well as misinterpretation). Let's amplify the definition. There are essentially four types of trendlines with which you should be familiar.

1. **Support Line**   A line connecting at least three nonconsecutive turning points on a bar chart, slanting in a horizontal

or upward direction and running under prices on the bar chart. Figure 3–1 shows several typical support lines.

2. **Resistance Line** A resistance line consists of at least three nonconsecutive turning points running above the price on a bar chart and slanting downward or horizontally. Figure 3–2 illustrates several support and resistance lines. Figure 3–3 shows some resistance lines.

In addition to the two basic types of trendlines there are two variations on trendlines.

Support Return Line The extension of a support line into the future after the trendline has been penetrated, in order to determine possible future price resistance.

Resistance Return Line The extension of a resistance line into the future once it has been penetrated by price in order to determine possible future support. Examples of support and resistance return lines are given in Figures 3–4, 3–5, and 3–6. Note how prices often come back to their return lines after penetration.

IMPLEMENTATION

There are various ways in which trendlines can be implemented in a trading program. Traditionally, they are used as indications for buying and selling based upon the belief that once a trendline has been penetrated in one direction or another, an important price move is likely to continue in the direction of the penetration. This is, of course, not always the case, but trendlines do appear to have validity as penetration points for buying and selling.

Trendlines have been used in several other ways. Many traders will turn bearish on the market when its support line has been penetrated to the downside. Prior to such penetration, however, traders will use the declines to the support line for going long on a market.

*What You Need to Know
about Trendlines*

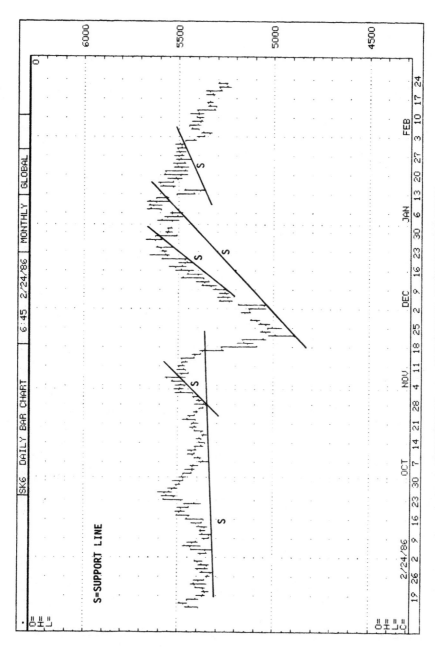

**FIGURE 3–1 VARIOUS SUPPORT LINES
(Reprinted with Permission of Commodity Quote Graphics)**

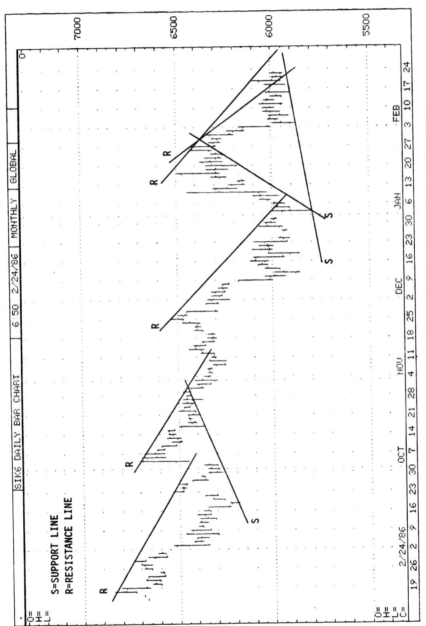

**FIGURE 3–2 VARIOUS SUPPORT AND RESISTANCE LINES
(Reprinted with Permission of Commodity Quote Graphics)**

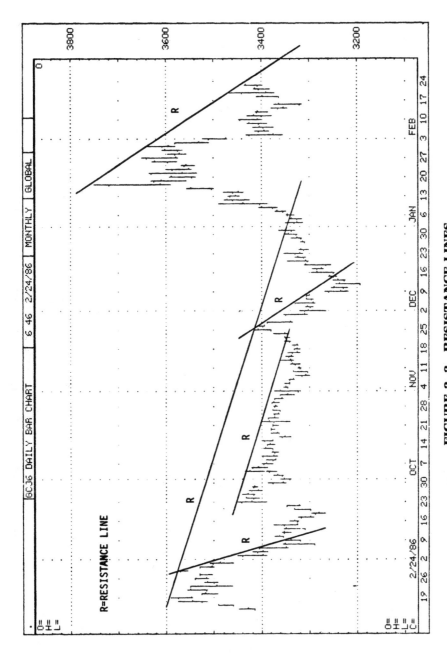

FIGURE 3–3 RESISTANCE LINES
(Reprinted with Permission of Commodity Quote Graphics)

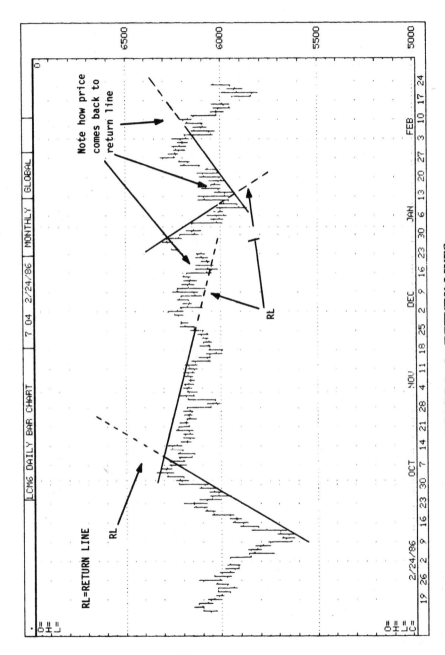

FIGURE 3-4 RETURN LINES

(Reprinted with Permission of Commodity Quote Graphics)

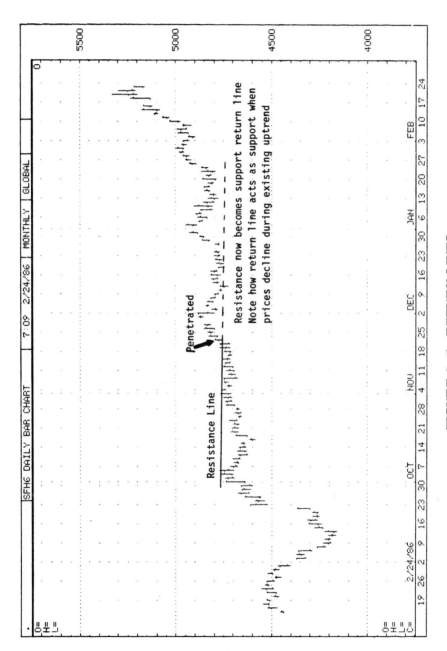

**FIGURE 3–5   RETURN LINES
(Reprinted with Permission of Commodity Quote Graphics)**

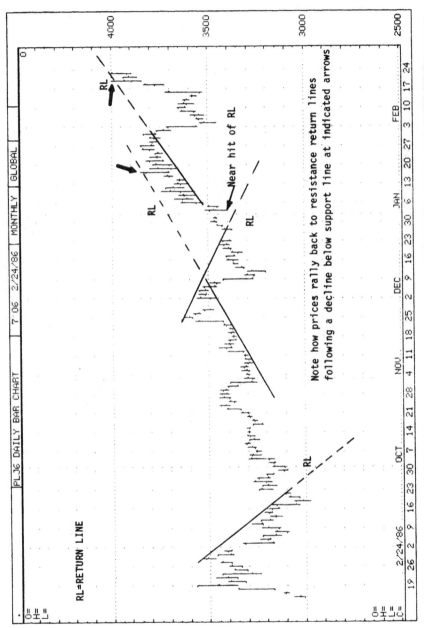

FIGURE 3–6   HOW RETURN LINES DEVELOP AS FUTURE SUPPORT AND/OR RESISTANCE
(Reprinted with Permission of Commodity Quote Graphics)

Alternatively, penetration of a resistance line is frequently taken to indicate a change in trend to the upside. Many traders will use the resistance lines points to establish short positions when a market rallies. Both techniques are commonly known and widely followed. It is difficult to state which procedure is the most reliable, but both have validity. Illustrations of all four applications are shown in Figures 3–7, 3–8, and 3–9.

SUGGESTIONS FOR APPLICATION

In recent years, trendline methods have been abandoned by many traders in favor of more sophisticated, but not necessarily more effective, computer-generated signals. Some of the more complex approaches will be discussed in later chapters. Based on my experience and observations in the markets, the trendline technique of buying on reactions to trendline support during an uptrend and selling on rallies to trendline resistance during a downtrend is a very effective technique.

The main considerations in trendline analysis are not primarily those of accurate signals, but rather accurate interpretation of signals. There is a tendency by trendline followers to adapt trendlines to fit their particular needs or market bias. This temptation must be avoided. One should attempt to adhere as strictly as possible to trendline rules. Here are some suggestions as to how you might implement the trendline technique.

1. The single most important rule is to trade with the trend. This is the most frequently stated, but most commonly misunderstood and overlooked aspect of successful speculation. Determining the major trend is not an especially difficult task, even for the novice trader. See Chapter 4 for detailed discussion on trend determination.
2. Assuming you have determined the major trend of prices and assuming that trend is up, the next step would be to draw support lines under the market.
3. Extend the trendlines into the future.

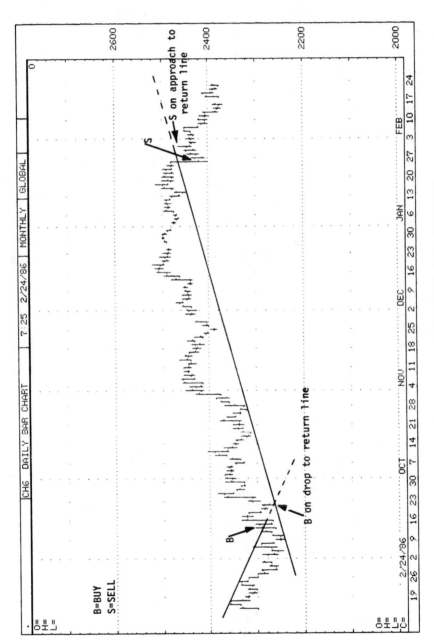

FIGURE 3-7   TRENDLINES AND SIGNALS

(Reprinted with Permission of Commodity Quote Graphics)

What You Need to Know
about Trendlines

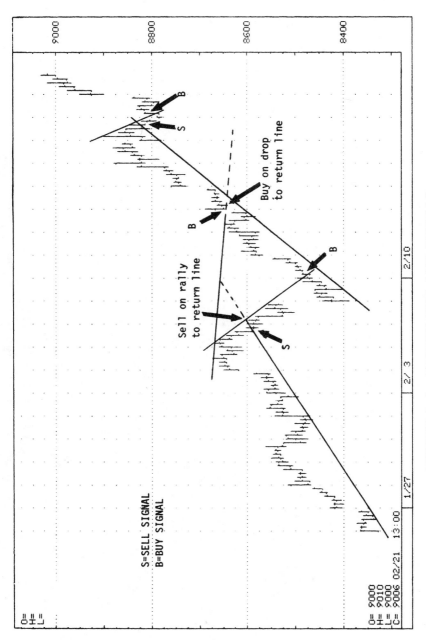

FIGURE 3–8 TRENDLINES AND SIGNALS
(Reprinted with Permission of Commodity Quote Graphics)

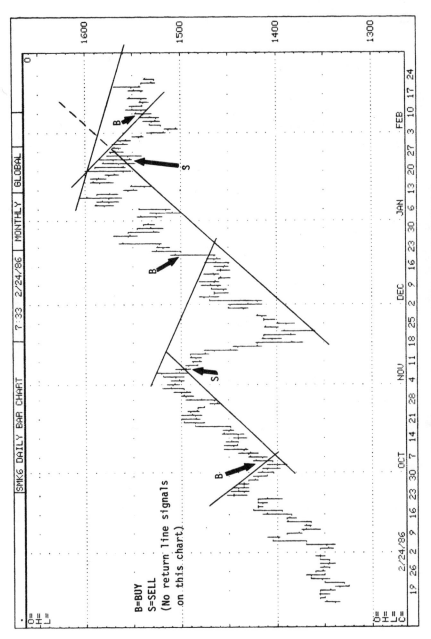

FIGURE 3-9 TRENDLINES AND SIGNALS
(Reprinted with Permission of Commodity Quote Graphics)

4. Determine the intersection point of trendline and price for the next market period (i.e., day, hour, etc.). Enter your price order slightly above the support line. I suggest a little leeway in order entry since many other traders will probably be entering their orders at or about the trendline price.

5. A good rule of thumb regarding stop losses is to liquidate your position as soon as your price has closed below the trendline, thereby negating its value as support and generating a reversing signal. Those willing to take a slightly greater risk can wait for two consecutive closings below the trendline, provided the first closing below the trendline does not exceed their maximum permissible per-trade losses (if such a limit is being used).

6. You can determine your objective in any of several ways. One technique is to reverse positions once a new trendline signal has formed. Another method is to sell your positions once a resistance line has been touched or approached. In the absence of a resistance line, other techniques could be used in liquidating a position, such as successively changing stops as the price continues to move in your favor (known as a trailing stop). The reverse procedure would hold true for selling short on the penetration of support.

As an aside, I would like you to remember that all of my examples are drawn from real time and represent real market situations. I could have chosen very carefully many examples illustrating "ideal" or "perfect" situations. Since the perfect situation is the exception rather than the rule, I have given you as many current time examples as possible.

USE OF TRENDLINES ON INTRADAY DATA

Trendline analysis can also be effective on intraday price data. Ideally, a half-hour or 15-minute price chart of active markets is best for this purpose. Support, resistance and trendline returns can be implemented on an intraday time scale. Illustrations of these techniques on intraday price charts are shown in Figures 3–10, 3–11 and 3–12.

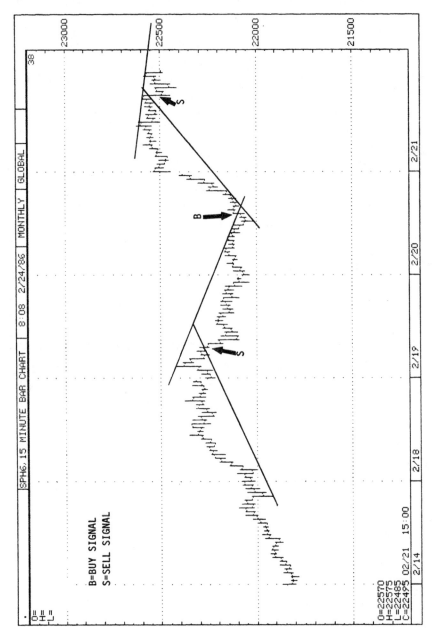

**FIGURE 3–10 TRENDLINE SIGNALS ON INTRADAY DATA
(Reprinted with Permission of Commodity Quote Graphics)**

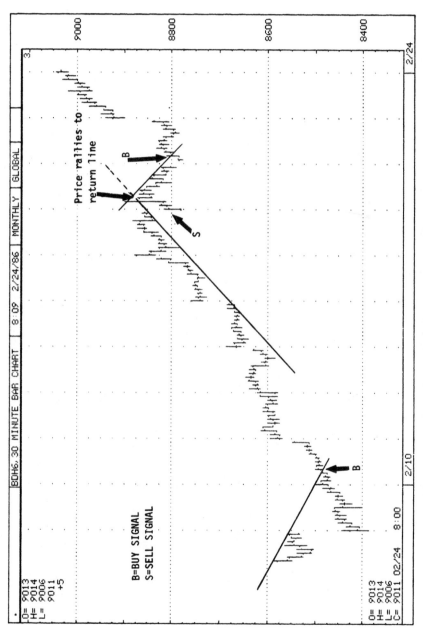

FIGURE 3–11 TRENDLINE SIGNALS ON INTRADAY DATA
(Reprinted with Permission of Commodity Quote Graphics)

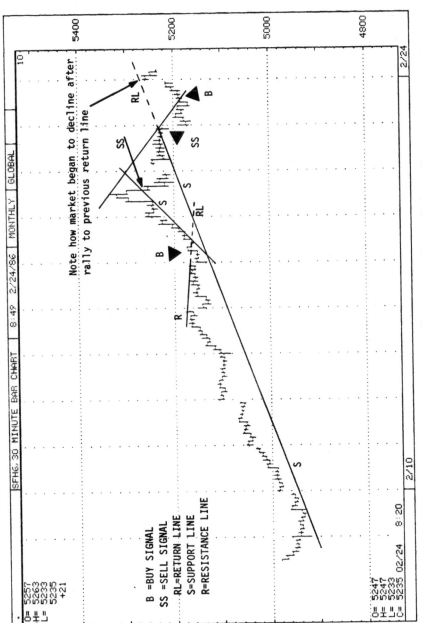

FIGURE 3-12 TRENDLINE SIGNALS ON INTRADAY DATA
(Reprinted with Permission of Commodity Quote Graphics)

Finally, as a point of information, Figures 3–13 and 3–14 show trendline analysis on a one-minute open/high/low/close price chart for those individuals who are considering using trendline analysis on extremely short-term time frames.

SUMMARY

1. Trendline analysis is a viable technique that seems to have considerably less following in recent years due to the advent of more complex mathematical approaches requiring computer analysis.
2. There are at least four different types of trendline signals, each adaptable to specific situations.
3. Trendline analysis is probably a desirable technique since it is not practiced by as many traders today as has been the case in the past.
4. Trendline analysis can provide exit and entry points based on support and resistance within existing trends.
5. Trendline analysis is reasonably objective and can be applied in a fairly consistent fashion provided simple objective rules are followed.
6. Trendline trading does not require complex interpretations or sophisticated equipment. It is, therefore, ideal for the newcomer.
7. Trendline trading can be used on daily and/or intraday data.

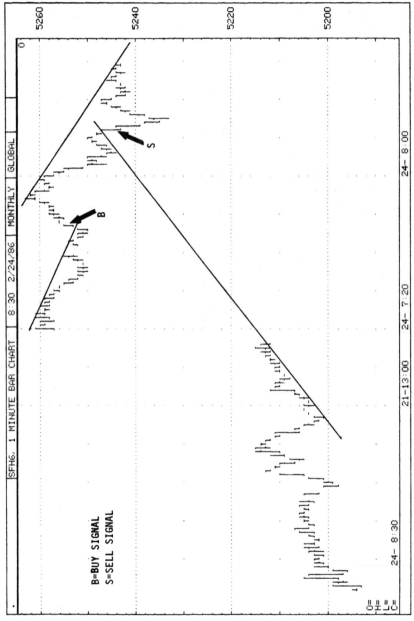

FIGURE 3–13 TRENDLINE SIGNALS ON ONE-MINUTE CHART
(Reprinted with Permission of Commodity Quote Graphics)

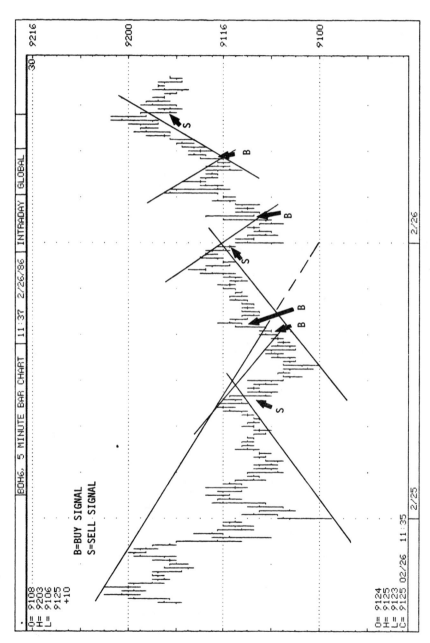

**FIGURE 3–14 TRENDLINE SIGNALS ON FIVE-MINUTE CHART
(Reprinted with Permission of Commodity Quote Graphics)**

Chapter
4

What You Should Know about Cycles

The cyclic method of analysis and forecasting has its roots in the work of Edward R. Dewey, founder of The Foundation for the Study of Cycles. Dewey's original work was in the cash commodity markets, as well as in the stock market. The use of price cycles has been popularized in recent years with the advent of computer technology and its ease of access to the speculating public. Yet, it does not have many followers today.

Let me preface my remarks about price cycles by saying that for the new traders, the cyclic technique is probably somewhat complicated and not initially recommended. Though I have been a proponent of cyclic trading for many years, I can say in all honesty that the application of cycles is not nearly as simple a matter as is the demonstration of their existence.

It is relatively simple to find price cycles, even if your experience in the futures markets is limited. A number of techniques may be employed to find cycles in futures and futures options. Some of the basic timing indicators used with cyclic price patterns can help you do extremely well. However, the intricacies of cyclic analysis are such that a commitment must be made and kept in order to achieve lasting success.

WHAT IS A CYCLE?

Stated simply, a price cycle is the tendency for price to repeat up and down trends in a relatively predictable fashion over a prescribed period of time. In other words, it is possible to state with fairly good accuracy that corn prices have a price cycle of approximately 5.7 years. This price cycle is illustrated in Figure 4–1. Within the 5.7-year price cycle for corn, there are also 30- to 34-month price cycles.

Price cycles are measured low to low, high to high or low to high. Various types of measurements are possible. A more thorough understanding of price cycles, timing indicators and cyclic theories may be obtained from my book, *The Handbook of Commodity Cycles: A Window on Time*[1]. Examples of various price cycles are provided in Figures 4–2 through 4–5.

MANY DIFFERENT CYCLES

Futures and cash prices demonstrate many different cyclic lengths ranging from the ultra-long term to the ultra-short term. On the short-term end of the spectrum, we have the approximately four- to five-day cycle in silver prices. On the long-term end of the continuum, we have the approximate 54-year cycle found in most commodity prices. This is about the longest cycle commodity traders study.

For the purpose of trading, cycle lengths from as long as 9 to 11 months to as short as 14 days are preferable. Most trading will likely be done on the basis of the approximate 25- to 32-day cycles. Figure 4–6 shows a listing of recent cycle low/high dates, cycle lengths, and specific markets. Note that these are subject to change.

[1]J. Bernstein, *The Handbook of Commodity Cycles: A Window on Time* (New York: John Wiley & Sons, 1982).

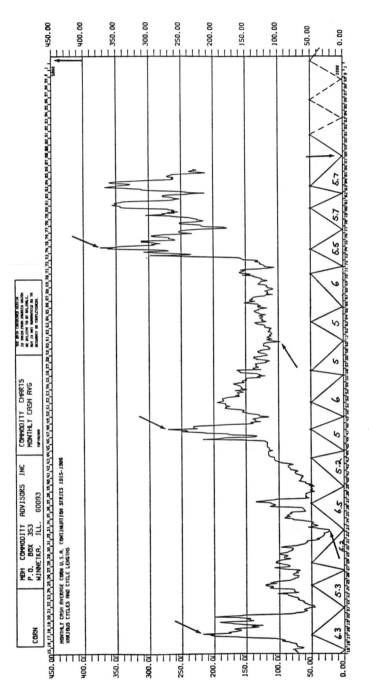

FIGURE 4–1 5.7-YEAR CORN PRICE CYCLE-(Arrows Show Longer Term Cycles)

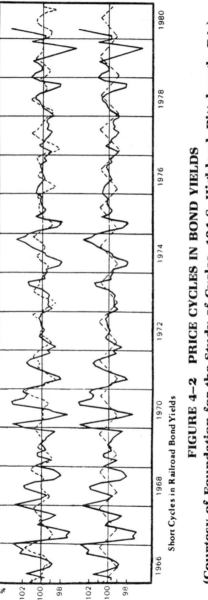

FIGURE 4-2   PRICE CYCLES IN BOND YIELDS

(Courtesy of Foundation for the Study of Cycles, 124 S. Highland, Pittsburgh, PA.)

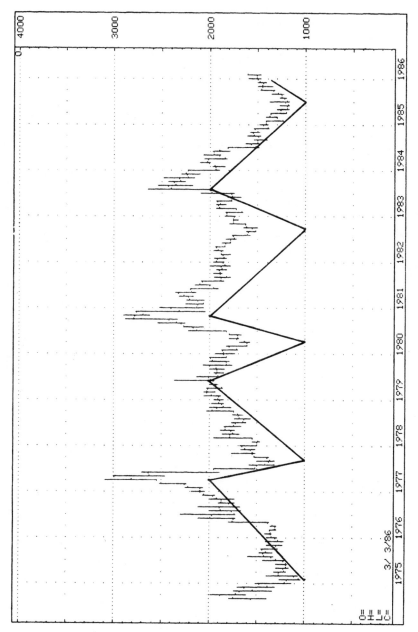

FIGURE 4-3 PRICE CYCLES IN SOYBEAN MEAL FUTURES
(Reprinted with Permission of Commodity Quote Graphics.)

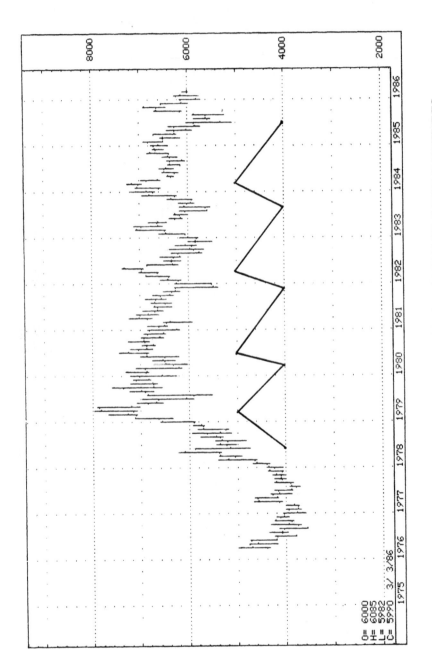

**FIGURE 4–4   APPROXIMATE 20-MONTH CYCLE IN CATTLE FUTURES
(Reprinted with Permission of Commodity Quote Graphics.)**

MARKET	MONTH	LT	HIGH / LOW		IT	HIGH / LOW		ST	HIGH / LOW	
LvCattle	Apr	10.2	1985	1985	45	12/85	07/85	32	01/27	02/19
LvHogs	Apr	1.7	1982	1985	45	12/85	09/85	28	01/27	02/18
PkBellies	May	1.7	1982	1985	45	12/85	08/85	28	01/27	due
Corn	May	2.8	1983	due	43	04/85	09/85	54	12/18	due
Oats	May	3.0	1983	due	43	03/85	due	40	12/31	02/20
Soybeans	May	2.8	1983	due	46	03/85	11/85	54	01/07	due
Soymeal	May	2.8	1983	1985	46	10/84	09/85	54	01/09	02/04
Soyoil	May	4.1	due	1984	46	04/85	12/85	54	12/17	due
Wheat	May	2.8	1983	1985	55	04/85	08/85	54	12/12	02/20
Cotton	May	5.9	1980	----	43	04/85	08/85	43	01/22	01/30
HtgOil	May	---	----	----	41	11/85	06/85	28	12/30	due
Lumber	May	4.0	1983	due	42	05/85	08/85	26	12/16	02/05
Sugar	May	6.2	1980	1985	56	10/85	06/85	56	12/02	01/14
O.J.	May	3.1	1984	due	35	01/85	due	60	12/17	02/24
Cocoa	May	3.7	1978	1982	44	12/85	03/85	54	01/07	due
Coffee	May	6.7	1977	1981	55	02/85	07/85	30	01/07	02/04
Copper	May	5.9	1980	1985	45	04/85	09/85	38	01/14	02/11
Silver	May	5.5	1980	1982	45	03/85	12/85	38	01/16	due
Gold	Apr	6.3	1980	1982	45	08/85	12/85	38	01/16	02/14*
Platinum	Apr	5.5	1980	1982	40	11/85	03/85	38	02/25*	02/04
Palladium	Jun	5.5	1980	1982	40	08/85	07/85	38	01/16	02/04*
TBills	Jun	4.5	due	1981	21	due	03/85	29	02/04	02/20
TBonds	Jun	4.5	due	1981	21	due	07/85	29	due	02/20
SwFranc	Jun	3.0	1980	due	41	due	02/85	41	due	01/13
DMark	Jun	3.0	1980	due	41	due	02/85	41	due	01/13
BrPound	Jun	6.1	1980	due	43	due	02/85	42	due	02/04
JYen	Jun	5.9	1978	due	43	due	02/85	42	due	12/03
CDollar	Jun	5.9	1980	due	21	10/85	09/85	21	02/24*	02/04
S&PIndex	Jun	4.0	due	1982	23	01/86	due	23	Uncertain	

Explanatory Notes: LT=Long Term Cycle Length measured in years and fractions. IT=
Intermediate Term Cycle Length measured in weeks. ST=Short Term Cycle Length measured
in market days. All cycles are measured in weeks. ST cycles are measured in market
days not calendar days. Cycle lengths are approximate and subject to change over time.
Dates listed are tentative and subject to change when more data becomes available.
"——" indicates that our research has not yet revealed any cycles of reliability or that
our data base is too limited. Cycles are not necessarily symmetrical.

**FIGURE 4–5 SAMPLE CYCLE LOW/HIGH DATES, LENGTHS, AND
TRENDS**

Price cycles are not perfect inasmuch as they can vary considerably in length. At times there will be an inversion of cyclic highs and lows with tops being made when lows should be made. This tends to occur at major turning points in the markets. For the purposes of this discussion we will concern ourselves with 9- to 11-month cycles and 14- to 60-day cycles.

APPLICATION OF THE THEORY

The application of the price cycles to futures trading consists of three elements: (1) Cycle Projections, (2) Projection and (3) Timing Entry.

First, if you do not know the cycle length for a given market you must research it in any of several ways. There are computer programs that will help you find cycles by matching dates and cycle lengths and testing them in the past, as well as projecting them into the future. Once you know the cycle length, the second element is to forecast the next approximate high or low. This is done simply by counting forward in time and establishing a time frame or time window during which the cycle should ideally top or bottom. See Figure 4–6 for an illustration. Once you have determined the ideal time frame of the next low or high, what I call the "time window," you will wait for the market to enter this time frame and, regardless of price, you act upon the timing indicator or timing signal, which allows you to enter with the anticipation of high probability of success.

TIMING INDICATORS

The use of timing indicators is possible during the optimum time frame for a top or bottom in the cycle. I have used several traditional and not-so-traditional tools. On the traditional side, we have the three basic timing signals I advanced in greater detail in my book, *The Handbook of Commodity Cycles: A Window on*

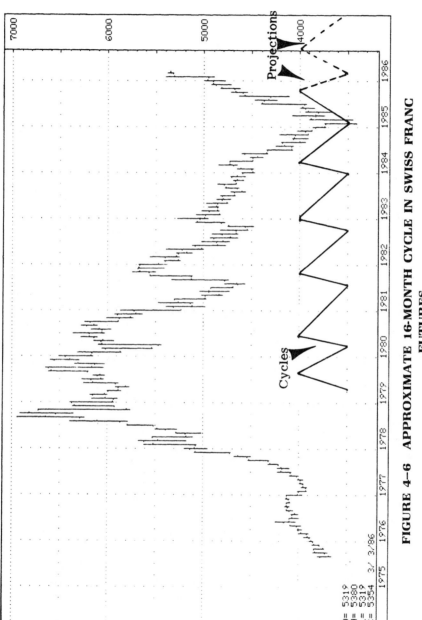

**FIGURE 4–6 APPROXIMATE 16-MONTH CYCLE IN SWISS FRANC
FUTURES**

(Reprinted with Permission of Commodity Quote Graphics)

Time.[2] The three basic indicators are shown in Figures 4–7, 4–8, and 4–9.

CYCLIC TRADING RULES

Although there are many different approaches to cycles and applications of cyclic theory, some general rules can help you in your study and application of cycles in the futures markets. Here is a summary of those rules:

1. **Find a market that has reliable cycles.** Currently, in 1986, some of these cycles are the 20–23-week cycle in stock index futures, the approximately 14-day cycle in stock index futures, the 50–60-day cycle in soybean futures, the 9–11-month cycle in all grain and livestock markets, the approximately 28-day cycle in silver and gold and the approximately 32-day cycle in interest rate futures. As market conditions change, cycles become more or less reliable and certain markets begin to exhibit better or worse cyclic tendencies. Therefore, continue to study the markets in order to isolate markets best traded using cycles.
2. **Attempt not to trade more than two or three markets** at once based on cycles.
3. **Do not duplicate markets.** What I mean here is don't trade several different markets that are closely related and that follow the same basic cycles (i.e., silver and gold, cattle and hogs, soybeans and soybean meal).
4. **Once you have determined the above information, keep your price charts up to date** and mark your cycles according to the rules provided in this chapter.
5. **Project the next cyclic** top or bottom as I have illustrated (Figure 4–5).
6. **Once you have entered the ideal cyclic time frame of a top or bottom,** examine timing signals and/or various timing indicators to pinpoint as closely as possible the next market turn.
7. **Use stop losses** specific to each trading signal.
8. **Attempt to develop a trailing stop procedure** by which you continually adjust your stop once you are in a profitable position. This is done so that not too much profit is lost back to the market if prices turn against you.

[2]J. Bernstein, *The Handbook of Commodity Cycles.*

Upside Reversal: Used for buying in cycle low time

Downside Reversal: Used for selling in cycle high time

If H_1 = high of day 1   And H_2 = high of day 2
L_1 = low of day 1 L_2 = low of day 2
And C_1 = closing price of day 1 C_2 = closing price of day 2

Then upside reversal is

$$L_2 < L_1 \quad and \quad C_2 > C_1 = R\ +$$

The downside reversal is

$$H_2 > H_1 \quad and \quad C_2 < C_1 = R\ -$$

Upside Reversal (R +) If today's low price is less than yesterday's low price and today's closing price is more than yesterday's closing price, then a daily upside reversal has been made.

Downside Reversal (R −) If today's high price is more than yesterday's high price and today's closing price is less than yesterday's closing price, then a daily downside reversal has been made.

**FIGURE 4.7 BASIC INDICATORS—
UPSIDE AND DOWNSIDE REVERSALS**

High Low Close Used for Selling in Cycle High Time (HLC)

Low High Close Signal Used for Buying in Cycle Low Time (LHC)

Close on low is defined as close at or within 10% of low. Close on high is defined as close at or within 10% of high. Both signals must occur on consecutive time periods in the time frame for the cycle turn.

FIGURE 4–8 BASIC INDICATORS—
LOW/HIGH CLOSE AND HIGH/LOW CLOSE TIMING SIGNALS

3H Indicator Used for Buying in Cycle Low Time

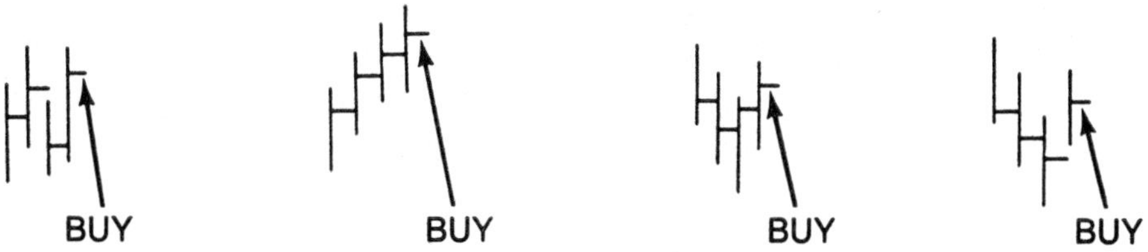

BUY   BUY   BUY   BUY

3L Indicator Used for Selling in Cycle High Time

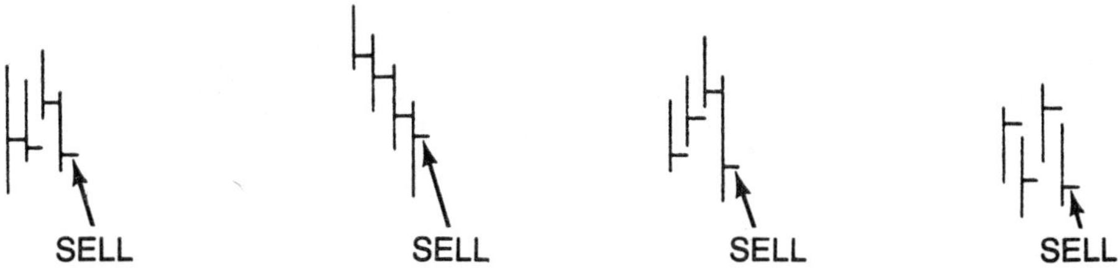

SELL   SELL   SELL   SELL

3H is defined as 4th close above highest of last three closes.

3L is defined as 4th close below lowest of last three closes.

**FIGURE 4.9 BASIC INDICATORS—
3H/3L TIMING INDICATORS**

SUMMARY

The cyclic method of futures trading is viable, but not recommended for novice traders. Used with an effective approach to timing and a sensible method of money management, this approach is capable of generating good profits over the short and long term. The use of figures options can improve cyclic timing by allowing more time within the ideal top and bottom time frames.

Chapter
5

What You Need to Know about Moving Averages

In the 1950s, Richard Donchain advanced the notion that a different type of trendline could be used to establish buy and sell signals, as well as indications of support and resistance. Rather than the familiar (straight-line) trend method, Donchain advanced the notion that a moving average of price could be constructed in order to provide market timing indicators.

A moving average is a simple mathematical manipulation of raw data that provides up-to-date or moving indications of market activity. Instead of examining price highs and lows for the entire history of the current contract, moving average constantly progresses and examines only a defined segment of time, particularly in the recent past.

A 10-day moving average, for example, will only look at prices for the last ten days, ignoring what has transpired before. In so doing, it provides a more sensitive measure by taking an average of the last ten days worth of prices, and on the 11th day dropping the oldest day in the data and recalculating the average with the current daily data. At any given point and time, only 10 days of data are used. However, they are the most recent 10 days.

Theoretically, price movement above the moving average is

considered bullish. If a market has been in an uptrend and then falls below the moving average line, this is taken to indicate a probable change in trend from bullish to bearish. Conversely if the market has been moving down (i.e., below moving average) and if it then crosses above its moving average, this is taken to be a bullish signal.

Although relatively simple to understand and straightforward in its construction and interpretation, the moving average has undergone many changes both in construction and application during the last 30 years. In only a few cases have the changes and additional effort been fruitful.

Figures 5–1, 5–2, 5–3, and 5–4 show several markets plotted with moving averages of different lengths. You will observe that the vertical lines show the opening high/low price bars and that the dotted smooth line shows the moving average plot. Observe my notes and comments.

Although the selection of one moving average as a means of timing entry and exit is certainly a technique which appears to have potential, it has been found that two moving averages, and perhaps three, tend to serve the purpose better. Whereas, one moving average will only indicate the trend over a specific length of time, the addition of one or two moving average indicators could significantly improve results by providing several measures of market strength or weakness.

Theoretically, buy signals are generated when two moving average lines cross in the upward direction, and sell signals are generated when two moving averages cross in the downward direction. See Figures 5–5 and 5–6. Finally, a third moving average could be added to further verify timing or to provide more evidence of a change in trend.

The application of various moving averages to determine buy and sell indications has received considerable study over the years. Certain combinations in certain markets are optimum, and other combinations do not appear to be particularly fruitful. Specifically, the 4-, 9-, and 18-day moving averages seem to work best together. Figures 5–7, 5–8, and 5–9 show this combination, and the signals that can be generated from its application.

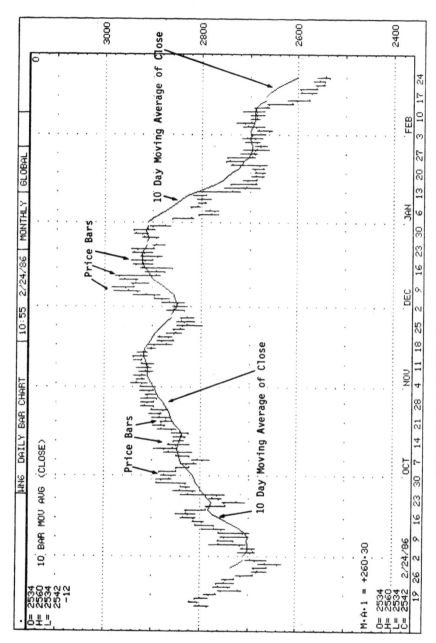

FIGURE 5-1 MOVING AVERAGES PLOTTED
(Reprinted with Permission of Commodity Quote Graphics)

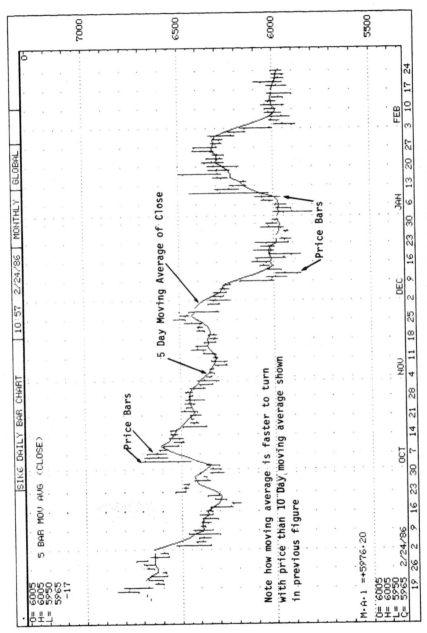

FIGURE 5–2 MOVING AVERAGES PLOTTED
(Reprinted with Permission of Commodity Quote Graphics)

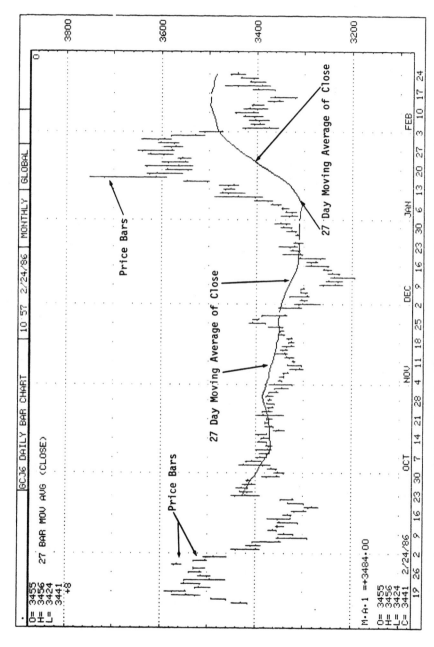

FIGURE 5-3 MOVING AVERAGES PLOTTED
(Reprinted with Permission of Commodity Quote Graphics)

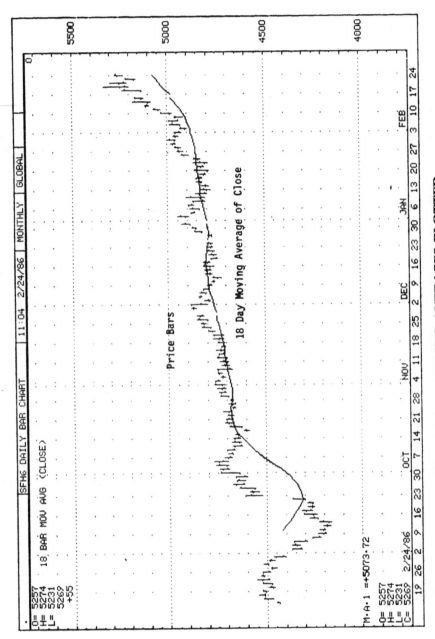

FIGURE 5-4 MOVING AVERAGES PLOTTED
(Reprinted with Permission of Commodity Quote Graphics)

What You Need to Know about
Moving Averages

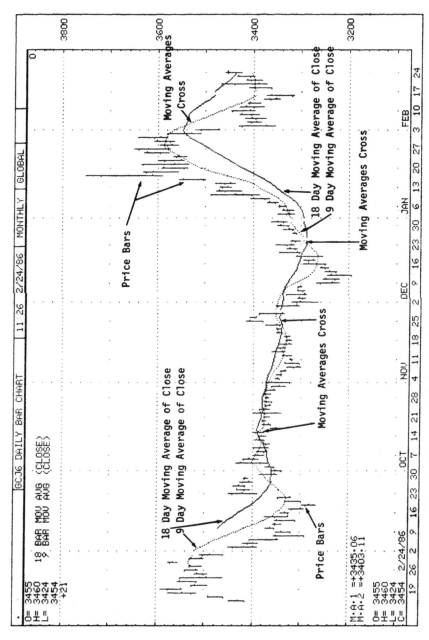

FIGURE 5-5 MOVING AVERAGES LINES CROSSING
(Reprinted with Permission of Commodity Quote Graphics)

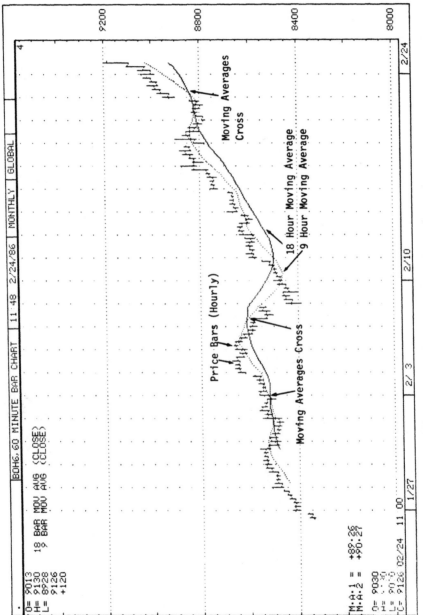

FIGURE 5-6 MOVING AVERAGES LINES CROSSING
(Reprinted with Permission of Commodity Quote Graphics)

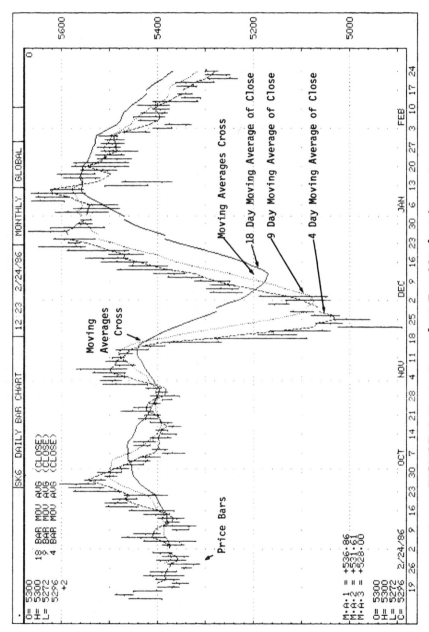

**FIGURE 5–7 4-, 9-, and 18-Day Moving Averages
(Reprinted with Permission of Commodity Quote Graphics)**

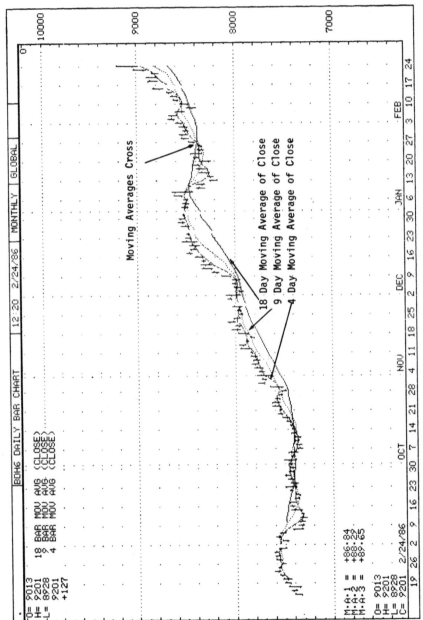

FIGURE 5–8 4, 9, AND 18-DAY MOVING AVERAGES
(Reprinted with Permission of Commodity Quote Graphics)

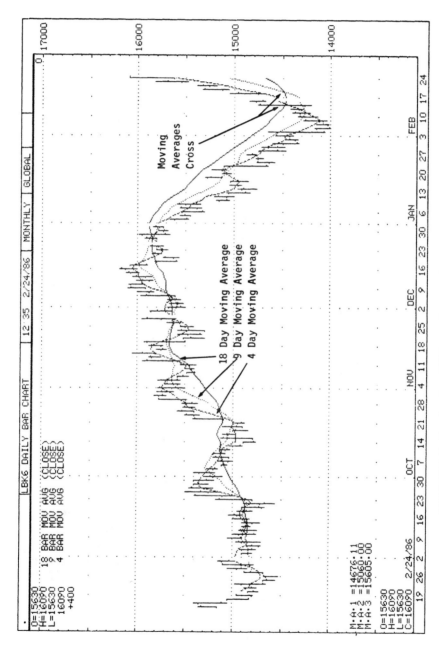

FIGURE 5–9   4-, 9-, AND 18-DAY MOVING AVERAGES
(Reprinted with Permission of Commodity Quote Graphics)

Moving average signals are popular among many money managers and speculators. Their popularity derives from the fact that moving average signals meet many of the specific criteria of effective systems. These are as follows:

1. Moving average signals are specific and objective.
2. Moving average signals can keep you in the market at all times: closing out a long, going short and covering a short when going long. This is valuable, since you will thus have a position when major moves begin.
3. Moving averages are trend-following systems. In other words, when a good trend is in effect, the likelihood of the moving average having a position consistent with the trend is very high.

Whatever combination of moving averages you may be using, the fact remains that moving averages are mechanical and easily implemented. Unfortunately, in certain types of markets, moving averages do not do well. These are primarily sideways or "choppy" markets in which prices may work back and forth in a small or large range, but over such a brief period of time that the moving average indicators are almost constantly out of phase with market activity. In such cases, the moving average system will not fare well, and, indeed, it may fare worse than most systems. However, in a trending market, moving average systems shine.

REVIEWING THE MOVING AVERAGE INDICATOR SIGNALS

1. Compute the moving average lengths.
2. Buy when all three moving averages have crossed in an upward direction. (If using one moving average then buy when price closes above the M.A.)
3. Sell and sell short when all three moving averages have crossed in a downward direction. (If using one moving average then sell when price closes below the M.A.)
4. Moving average systems are based upon reversals. In other words, when a long position is closed out, a short position is entered. When a short position is closed out, a long position is entered.

Moving average systems can be very helpful to the new trader. Though they may result in greater than acceptable risk, they do assist with self-discipline and money management. Before you consider using moving averages for trading study this approach *very thoroughly.* There are many variation on this theme, some much better than others.

SUMMARY

The general aspects of moving averages were discussed. Some specifics regarding moving average techniques were reviewed and illustrated. Strengths and weaknesses of traditional moving average systems were reviewed. The moving average systems available today are much more sophisticated and well-tested than they have been in the past. Consistent application of moving average techniques has validity as a successful methodology for technical traders. The use of such systems should not be discounted by novice traders inasmuch as these systems are specific, mechanical, trend following and relatively simple to follow. Though there can be large drawdowns and periods of persistent losses in zig zag ("whipsaw") type markets, the potential of moving average systems in trending markets is tremendous.

Chapter

6

What You Need to Know about Seasonality

Another form of cyclical price movement is seasonality. Seasonality refers to the tendency of prices to move in certain directions at certain times of the year. Some seasonal price tendencies are extremely reliable, having occurred in excess of 90 percent of the time over a span of many years. Other seasonals are less reliable.

In recent years, the popularity of trading in anticipation of seasonal price tendencies has grown partly as a result of computer use in analyzing large amounts of statistics used to isolate these tendencies. There are three different types of seasonal tendencies: (1) Cash Seasonality, (2) Futures Seasonality and (3) Futures Spread Seasonality.

CASH SEASONALITY

Each cash commodity market has its own seasonal tendency. If we study cash commodity prices over an extended period of time on a month-to-month change basis, we find that during certain months of the year, price tends to top, whereas during other months price tends to bottom. Furthermore, during certain times of the year uptrends are common while during other times of the year downtrends are common. Seasonality was described by W. D. Gann in some of his publications as far back as 1932. References are listed at the end of this chapter.

The technique of constructing or calculating a seasonal price tendency chart is very simple. The procedure is as follows:

1. List the monthly cash average prices in tabular form.
2. Calculate the differences from one month to the next for the entire period of data.
3. List the differences in columns according to month, for example January to February differences, February to March differences, March to April differences.
4. Add the month to month differences for each year back to the start of your data.
5. Take the average of your differences.
6. Plot the first average. Add it to the second average of difference and plot this figure. Do so until you have plotted all 12 months of differences.
7. Calculate the percentage of time during the history of your data that prices are up or down for a given month. What you will arrive at is a chart that looks like Figure 6–1.

Cash price seasonal tendencies will allow you to determine when markets are likely to be their strongest or weakest, and when markets usually top or bottom. They do not, however, have much applicability for the short-term trader. Their primary use is for the producer, hedger, or long-term trader. Figures 6–2 through 6–5 show some cash seasonals for various markets.

SEASONAL FUTURES TENDENCIES

An approach much more suited to the needs of the short-term trader is the use of seasonal futures tendencies on a week-to-week or day-to-day basis. Several approaches can be used in analyzing weekly and daily seasonal futures tendencies. Essentially, the approach is very similar to what has been described earlier for monthly seasonal tendencies in the cash market, however, in this

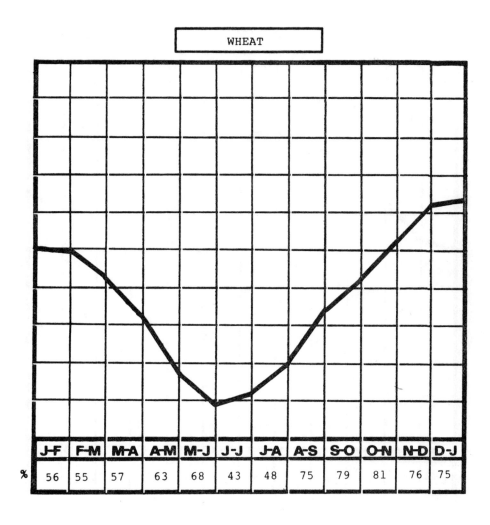

J-F	F-M	M-A	A-M	M-J	J-J	J-A	A-S	S-O	O-N	N-D	D-J
56	55	57	63	68	43	48	75	79	81	76	75

FIGURE 6–1   CASH SEASONALITY IN WHEAT (1936-1983)

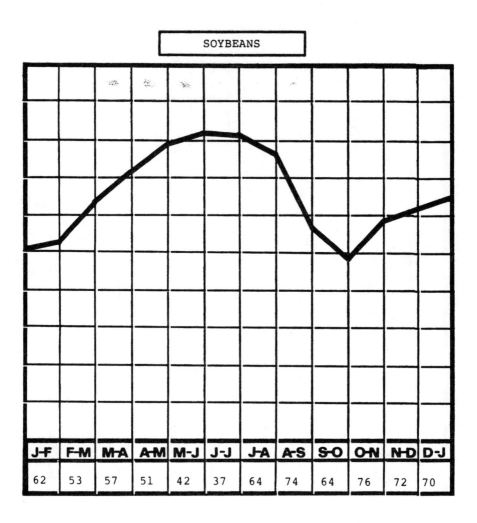

SOYBEANS											
J-F	F-M	M-A	A-M	M-J	J-J	J-A	A-S	S-O	O-N	N-D	D-J
62	53	57	51	42	37	64	74	64	76	72	70

FIGURE 6–2   CASH SEASONAL PRICE TENDENCY IN SOYBEANS

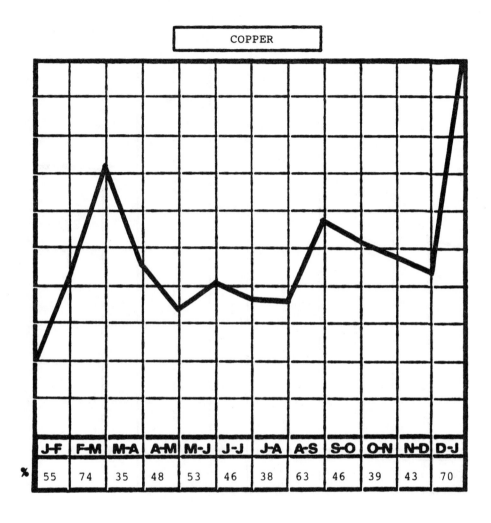

	J-F	F-M	M-A	A-M	M-J	J-J	J-A	A-S	S-O	O-N	N-D	D-J
%	55	74	35	48	53	46	38	63	46	39	43	70

FIGURE 6–3   CASH SEASONAL PRICE TENDENCY IN COPPER

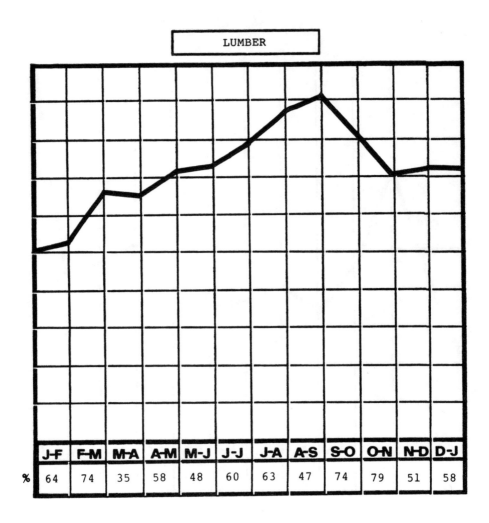

LUMBER											
J-F	F-M	M-A	A-M	M-J	J-J	J-A	A-S	S-O	O-N	N-D	D-J
64	74	35	58	48	60	63	47	74	79	51	58

FIGURE 6–4   CASH SEASONAL PRICE TENDENCY IN LUMBER

What You Need to Know about
Seasonality

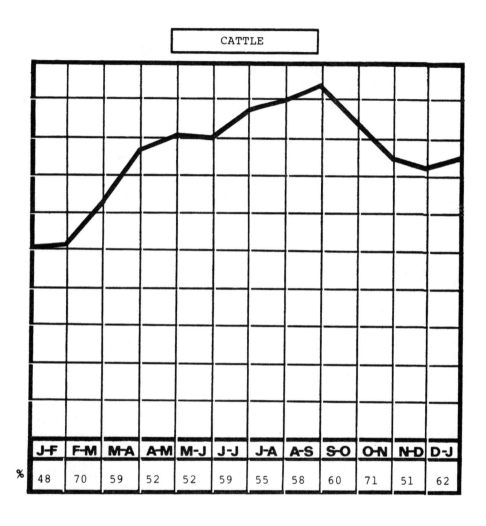

CATTLE

J-F	F-M	M-A	A-M	M-J	J-J	J-A	A-S	S-O	O-N	N-D	D-J
48	70	59	52	52	59	55	58	60	71	51	62

%

**FIGURE 6–5   CASH SEASONAL PRICE TENDENCY
IN CATTLE (BEEF STEERS)**

case weekly or daily data are used.

Seasonal futures tendencies are specific to the futures contract month. When we analyze the statistics, for each futures contract month, we arrive at a chart that looks like Figure 6–6. As you can see, the seasonal futures tendency of copper shows that prices usually begin moving higher in January and peak in April. The statistics inside the box at the bottom of the chart show the percentage of times the prices moved up or down for the given week over the time frame studied. In other words, it is possible to determine when one should ideally be long or short in a given market based on the history of that market.

This is not to say that the seasonals shown will always be correct. Certainly there is a degree of probability, however, they do *tell you the usual market tendency at given times of the year.* By using these tendencies you can frequently avoid the wrong side of the market. You can keep on the right side of the market more often.

Furthermore, you can "filter" the market by using a combined approach. Instead of following the weekly seasonal tendencies blindly, you could study the major market trend then follow only those weekly seasonal readings which go in the direction of the major trend.

In addition to weekly seasonal futures tendencies, it has been demonstrated that seasonality also exists on a day-to-day basis using early futures data. Figure 6–7 shows some of the statistics using calendar days change from December cotton futures. Observe that my arrows point to days that the given market has been up or down a high percentage of the time. Such short-term seasonal statistics can be generated on all markets with an appropriately long data base, however, the weekly approach I have described is best suited to most traders.

SEASONAL FUTURES SPREADS

The commodity spread or straddle has been previously described in Chapter 1. In addition to the use of a technical

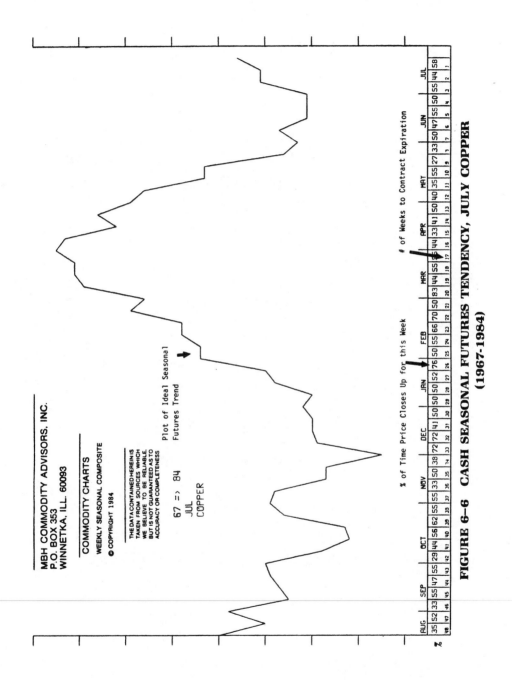

FIGURE 6–6 CASH SEASONAL FUTURES TENDENCY, JULY COPPER
(1967-1984)

DATE	% Days Up	% Days Down	Avg. +	Avg. -	DATE	% Days Up	% Days Down	Avg. +	Avg. -
SEP 22	50	50	0.35	0.57	OCT 25	63	37	0.66	0.85
SEP 23	50	50	0.27	0.36	OCT 26	50	50	0.23	0.55
SEP 24	58	42	0.48	0.87	OCT 27	53	47	0.38	0.36
SEP 25	50	50	0.54	0.75	OCT 28	58	42	0.24	0.48
SEP 26	41	59	0.30	0.69	OCT 29	58	42	0.54	0.37
SEP 27	58	42	0.72	0.26	OCT 30	66	34	0.41	0.78
SEP 28	66	34	0.31	0.50	OCT 31	50	50	0.49	0.26
SEP 29	53	47	0.36	0.46					
SEP 30	58	42	1.00	0.18	NOV 1	25	75	0.72	0.65
					NOV 2	40	60	0.34	0.31
OCT 1	50	50	0.52	0.89	NOV 3	33	67	0.52	0.60
OCT 2	50	50	0.46	0.85	NOV 4	66	34	0.59	0.06
OCT 3	66	34	0.61	0.53	NOV 5	40	60	0.70	0.39
OCT 4	50	50	0.12	0.45	NOV 6	63	37	0.22	0.67
OCT 5	83	17	0.40	0.08	NOV 7	66	34	0.52	0.41
OCT 6	61	39	0.51	0.50	NOV 8	54	46	0.96	0.34
OCT 7	41	59	0.76	0.57	NOV 9	33	67	0.40	0.33
OCT 8	45	55	0.43	0.55	NOV 10	46	54	0.31	0.55
OCT 9	63	37	0.64	0.44	NOV 11	45	55	0.60	0.76
OCT 10	50	50	0.43	0.40	NOV 12	41	59	0.08	0.51
OCT 11	54	46	0.24	1.15	NOV 13	41	59	0.42	0.61
OCT 12	58	42	0.54	0.55	NOV 14	41	59	0.56	0.62
OCT 13	83	17	0.27	1.02	NOV 15	50	50	0.55	0.70
OCT 14	33	67	0.07	0.84	NOV 16	41	59	0.25	0.44
OCT 15	33	67	0.56	0.46	NOV 17	61	39	0.58	0.45
OCT 16	58	42	0.35	0.22	NOV 18	41	59	0.39	0.36
OCT 17	58	42	0.64	0.64	NOV 19	41	59	0.51	0.43
OCT 18	58	42	0.38	0.56	NOV 20	58	42	0.81	0.61
OCT 19	33	67	0.57	0.75					
OCT 20	38	62	0.23	0.50					
OCT 21	58	42	0.61	0.49					
OCT 22	45	55	0.39	0.49					
OCT 23	41	59	0.23	0.65					
OCT 24	50	50	0.38	0.58					

FIGURE 6–7 SEASONAL STATISTICS USING CALENDAR DAYS—
Percent of Time Price was Up or Down for Given Market on Indi-
cated Calendar Day
During Time Period Studied in December Cotton Futures—Arrows
Show High Readings

analytical approach, spreads can be studied on the basis of seasonal tendencies. Some seasonal tendencies have been demonstrated to be highly predictable. It should be understood, however, that spreads are also affected by fundamental conditions such as government programs, supply, demand, interest rates, and carrying charges.

A seasonal spread tendency can be calculated in a fashion very similar to the weekly seasonal price tendency, however, one uses the three-weekly spread differences as opposed to the week-to-week futures contract differences. A composite seasonal spread chart showing one of the most repetitive seasonal spreads, long June cattle/short October cattle is shown in Figure 6–8.

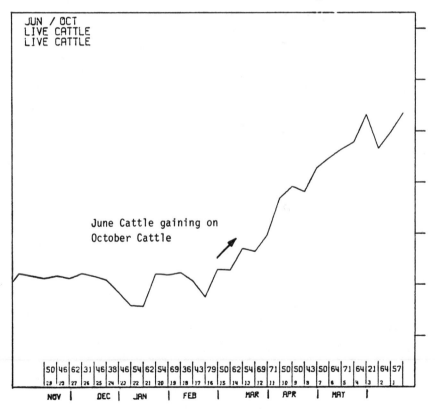

FIGURE 6-8   SEASONAL SPREAD TENDENCY:
JUNE VERSUS OCTOBER LIVE CATTLE

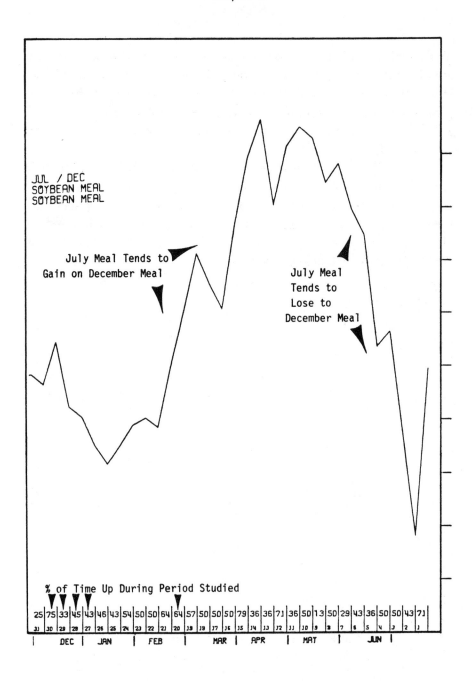

**FIGURE 6–9   SEASONAL SPREAD TENDENCY—
JULY VERSUS DECEMBER SOYBEAN MEAL**

Ideally, a speculator would enter long June cattle/short October cattle, buying October cattle, as shown on the chart. For most of the history of the live cattle futures contract at the Chicago Mercantile Exchange, this spread has shown a seasonal movement favoring June during the time period indicated a great majority of the time. Some other reliable seasonal spreads are shown in Figures 6–9, 6–10, 6–11, and 6–12.

There are several good techniques for seasonal trading that are not only simple to implement, but that can also yield very good results. The seasonal futures methods and the seasonal futures spread methods have good potential for novice traders, since they tend to keep you on the right side of the markets and since they help you trade in the direction of historically valid seasonals. Some rules to observe in implementing seasonal trades follow.

1. **Weekly Seasonal Trading:** Simple Use of Weekly Seasonal Tendencies.

    1. Isolate weekly seasonal tendencies which have high percentage of tendencies toward up or down moves (i.e., 75 percent or more).
    2. Enter position of the last trading day of the week prior to which the seasonal up or down move is likely to occur.
    3. Exit the trade during the last trading day of the week of the seasonal move.
    4. Alternatively, determine a profit objective based on support or resistance for the current price chart of the given commodity and month.
    5. Figures 6–13, 6–14, and 6–15 give specific examples of this approach.

2. **Filtered Weekly Seasonal Trading**

    1. Determine the trend of the market.
    2. If trend is up, then follow only those weekly percentage readings that are up for the given market and implement steps outlined in Item 1. Do the reverse for markets in downtrends. Specifically, take only those seasonal trades with high percentages on the downside.

3. **Seasonal Spread Trading**

1. Determine which seasonal spread tendencies are reliable.
2. Follow the same procedure outlined for the two techniques above, depending on the orientation and degree of risk you wish to take.

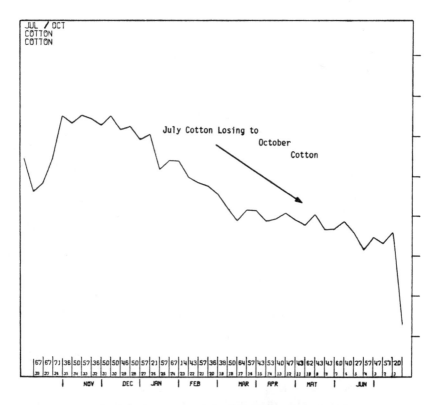

**FIGURE 6–10   SEASONAL SPREAD TENDENCY—
JULY VERSUS OCTOBER COTTON**

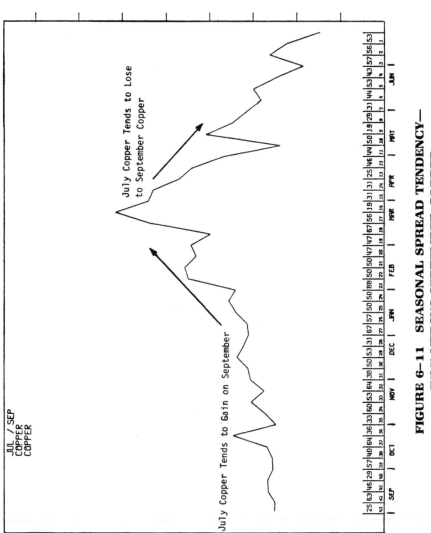

**FIGURE 6–11 SEASONAL SPREAD TENDENCY—
JULY VERSUS SEPTEMBER COPPER**

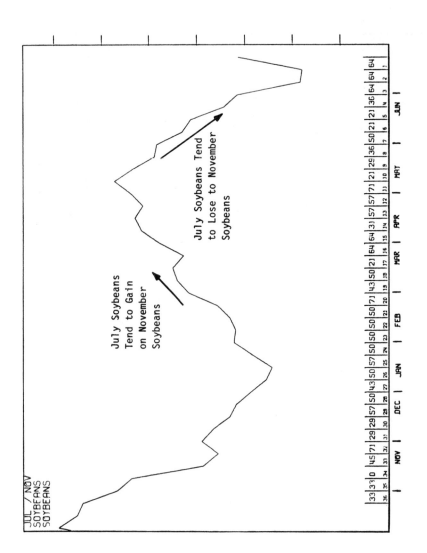

**FIGURE 6–12 SEASONAL SPREAD TENDENCY—
JULY VERSUS NOVEMBER SOYBEANS**

What You Need to Know about
Seasonality

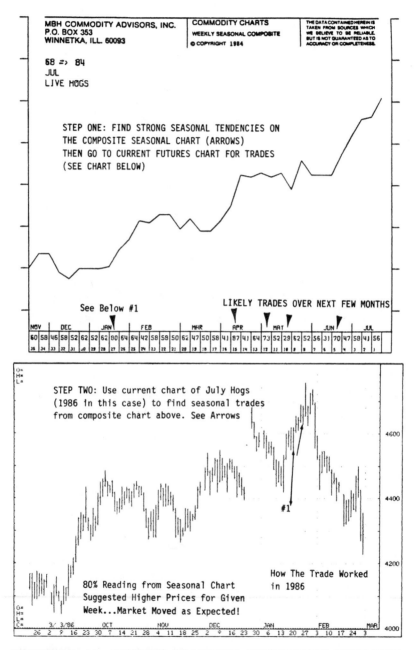

FIGURE 6–13   WEEKLY SEASONAL TENDENCIES USED FOR SHORT-TERM TRADING ON CURRENT CONTRACT
(Reprinted with Permission of Commodity Quote Graphics)

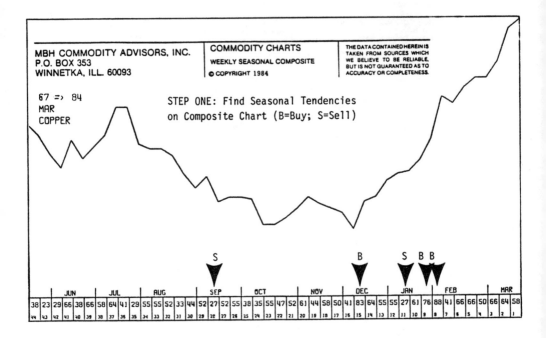

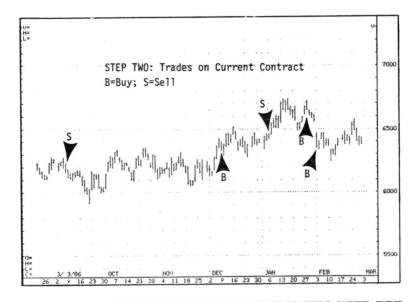

**FIGURE 6–14   WEEKLY SEASONAL TENDENCIES USED FOR
SHORT-TERM TRADING ON CURRENT CONTRACT
(Reprinted with Permission of Commodity Quote Graphics)**

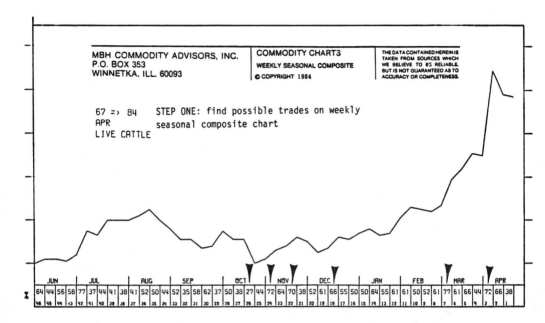

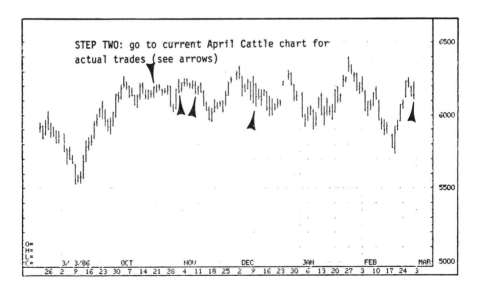

**FIGURE 6–15   WEEKLY SEASONAL TENDENCIES USED FOR
SHORT-TERM TRADING ON CURRENT CONTRACT
(Reprinted with Permission of Commodity Quote Graphics)**

SUMMARY

The existence of seasonal price tendencies in cash commodity prices, stocks, futures and futures spreads is a fact with which most traders are familiar. However, in spite of modern computer research studies, few traders are well-versed in this important approach to futures trading. Given the historical reliability of many seasonal price patterns, the beginning trader can take considerably less risk by learning how to use seasonals and by using them in his or her trading approach. There are many different seasonal tendencies and many different ways in which to employ them. Some are discussed in this chapter.

Inasmuch as seasonal data is relatively simple to obtain and relatively simple to evaluate, the value of seasonality in most trading approaches is significant. Yet, in spite of the high reliability of some seasonal price tendencies, many systems and traders still "buck the trend" refusing to acknowledge the importance of repetitive seasonal patterns in futures prices. I would go so far as to say that seasonality can be used as a good initial indicator, for some systems which, when combined with even the most elementary timing indicators can yield very good results. I encourage more traders to look in the direction of seasonality for potentially valuable trading methods and ideas.

Part 2

Discipline and Trading

Chapter
7

On Discipline: This Book's Most Important Chapter

Although there are many things I could tell you about different trading approaches and the lessons I have learned through long and hard experience, none of them would be more meaningful, ultimately, than the lessons I have learned about discipline. The advice I can give you about this single most important area of success in futures trading is the most important knowledge I can impart. If I were to suggest that you read only one chapter in this book, this would be it!

When asked what is the single most important variable to success in futures trading, my response is not "trading systems" nor is it "the type of computer you have" nor is it "the type of inside information to which you might be privy." It is not "the amount of capital you have" or "the broker with whom you are trading." The simple fact of the matter is that what ultimately separates winners from losers, commercial, speculative, short-term, long-term, or otherwise, is *discipline and its many facets.*

To most traders discipline is just another well-worn topic in futures trading. They have heard the word, they've studied the preachings and they believe they have learned the lessons. My observations and experiences with futures markets and futures traders leads me to the irreversible conclusion that *the lessons have not been learned!*

To most traders the word "discipline" merely signifies something they know they need and believe they have. In their hearts of hearts, however, most traders know they are sorely lacking in discipline, and that they will probably never have it.

Discipline is virtually impossible to teach and to learn from anyone else. It is complex, elusive, evasive and often camouflaged. It is the sine qua non of success in virtually every form of human achievement, in every field and in every generation. To the best of my knowledge there is no simple way to define discipline, nor is there any simple way to acquire or teach it.

There are futures traders who have virtually no objective trading system to speak of, but who, through the application and development of discipline, have achieved success. On the other hand, there are many futures traders with excellent trading systems, that for lack of discipline have remained unsuccessful, in spite of massive statistical evidence to suggest that their techniques are indeed valid and capable of producing tremendous profits.

Discipline can transform a marginal trading system into a highly successful one. Lack of discipline can transform a potentially successful trading system into a consistent and persistent losing approach. In reviewing the history, literature and facts about virtually any form of investing or speculating, I have found that a key element of success is discipline. It is impossible for me to overstate the fact that discipline is probably the main difference between winners and losers.

The purpose of this chapter is twofold. First to underscore the importance of discipline, and second, to suggest a number of ways by which discipline can be developed and improved. First, let's look at the fashion in which discipline functions, and at its ramifications in the successful trading approach.

WHY DISCIPLINE IS IMPORTANT

As you know, there are many different approaches to futures trading. Some are potentially more profitable than others. Some are simple, some are complex, some are logical, and some not so logical. Regardless of the trading approach one employs, all trading systems and methods have certain elements in common. These are as follows:

1. Specific signals (rules) for entry and exit.
2. Specific parameters, methods of calculation of timing signals.
3. Specific action that must be taken as a function of 1 and 2.

When systems and methods are tested by computer in order to generate hypothetical or "ideal" results, they are not tested in real time, but rather in theoretical time, with perfect adherence to the trading rules that have been programmed into the computer. What gets tested is a series of specific parameters. What comes out is a listing of trades and hypothetical results based on *the perfect execution of the rules that were programmed into the machine.*

The output of the system test will yield many different types of information including such things as percentage of trades profitable, percentage of trades unprofitable, percentage of trades that break even, average winning trade in dollars, average losing trade in dollars, performance for given markets, average length of time per trade, etc. All of the data derived from the computer test of a trading model is based upon perfect follow-up, implementation and execution of trading signals according to the parameters programmed into the computer. There is no room for error!

There is no room for lack of discipline! Some systems are profitable only 55–65 percent of the time. Other systems show higher percentages. But such statistics can be misleading. I have rarely seen systems that are profitable more than 80 percent of the time. Certainly you can imagine a trading system which is correct 90 percent of the time, making a $100 profit, on the average, each time, and then losing $900 on the occasion that it is wrong, would certainly not be very profitable. Furthermore, the individual trading the system would give back all of the profits made on nine trades on one losing trade! One losing trade would bring the account back to even. Should there be another error due to lack of discipline, the account would show a net loss.

Conversely, a trading system may show eight losers for every two winners. If, however, the average profitable trade is much larger than the average losing trade, even a system having nine losers out of every 10 trades could be profitable, if the bottom line per trade were higher on the winning side. Nevertheless, such a system would be thrown astray if lack of discipline resulted in much larger losses than expected for the eight losing trades. If lack of discipline interfered significantly with the profits on the two profitable trades, then the net results might be much worse than anticipated.

A third scenario would be a marginal trading system. Assume that a trading system is profitable about 65 percent of the time. In such cases, we can figure that approximately 65 out of every 100 trades are winners, and 35 are losers. You can see that only 30 percent separates the winners from the losers. In other words, the trader must have sufficient discipline to keep the losses as small as possible, and to maximize the profits. This is where discipline enters into the formula.

Discipline is the machinery which can make or break any trading system. There are some conditions under which discipline will not be the important variable, however, *in most cases it is the significant variable.* All of the glowing trading statistics for your trading system will be totally useless if you are not capable of duplicating the exact statistics generated by the computer test of your trading system. In other words, you must stick as close to the averages as possible or one or two losses, much larger than the average, or one or two profits much smaller than the average, will be sufficient to ruin your results. Sometimes this can occur strictly as a function of market behavior (i.e., limit moves against you) however, more often than not, as I have stated before, it is the trader who is responsible for maintaining the discipline of a system.

DOING YOUR "HOMEWORK"

It is uncanny how many times markets will begin major moves in line with the expectations of many advisors, analysts and speculators, without these various individuals being on board for the big move. Why do things like this happen? How often has this happened to you? I know from personal experience that many individuals have good records at predicting where prices will go. I also know that when it comes to doing their homework, they have especially poor records.

What do I mean by doing your homework? I mean very simply, keeping up to date on the signals generated by the system or systems you are following. In order to keep in touch with the markets according to your system, you will need to have a regular schedule for doing the technical or fundamental work your system requires. Whether this consists of simple charting that may take only five minutes per day, or complex mathematical calculations which may take considerably longer, the fact remains that the discipline of doing your homework is one of the prerequisites for successful trading.

If you have a system and do not follow it, you are guilty of poor discipline. If you have a system and fail to do the work which generates your trading signals, then you are just as guilty of lacking discipline. As you can see, and as you can well appreciate, it is a sad but true fact that most traders don't even get past the first step.

Can you identify strongly, or even partially with some of the things I am saying? How often have you been in the situation of missing a move because your charts or systems were not up to date? How many times has this frustrated you into making an unwarranted decision in an effort to compensate for your first error? If the truth were fully known, we would know that many of us are guilty. The sad fact about this situation is that its rectification is a very simple matter. In fact, the steps one must take in order to rectify virtually any problem resulting from lack of trading discipline are very specific, easily understood and exceptionally elementary to implement.

It is, unfortunately true that the discipline required to trade consistently and successfully is the same type of discipline that is required in virtually every aspect of human life. Whether it is the discipline that is required to lose weight, stop smoking or to develop a successful business, the roots and basics of all discipline are the same.

If you develop discipline in your trading, I am certain that it will spread to other areas of your life, including your personal affairs. Unfortunately, however, discipline in other aspects of your life may not be necessarily spread very quickly to your trading. The nature of futures trading provides serious challenges to discipline developed in other areas of life. Suggestions for improving discipline will be provided later on in this chapter.

HOW LACK OF DISCIPLINE GROWS STRONGER

Lack of discipline is not confined to any one situation, any one trade or any one trader. Lack of discipline, for all intents and purposes, is a way of life, albeit a bad one. Individuals who achieve success without adhering to certain disciplined practices do so as a stroke of good fortune, and stand the chance of forfeiting their wealth through a lack of disciplined action. Unfortunately, lack of discipline is not a simple matter, but rather it spreads like a cancerous growth through the trader's behavior. Lack of discipline tends to result in a compounding of errors that result in a far greater tragedy than that caused by the initial mistake itself. Yet, it should come as no surprise to those who understand relationships, whether they are those of individuals or those between the individual and the marketplace. In an interpersonal relationship, lack of discipline and specificity can cause negative interaction.

Negative interaction will then result in further tests of discipline and self-control. These will, in turn, result in other problems, failures and negative experiences until the entire relationship is threatened. The same is true of one's trading.

Lack of discipline in instituting a trade may frustrate the trader into a further display of poor discipline. After several such incidents the trader will become frustrated causing further errors to become likely. The net result is usually a succession of errors each compounding upon the other and each likely far worse than the previous. It is for this reason that one must take great care to avoid making even the first mistake due to a lack of discipline. The first mistake will lead to the second, the second may lead to four others and four others may lead to 16 others. This is the manner in which a lack of discipline tends to spread. Frequently it can grow at an exponential rate.

SUGGESTIONS FOR IMPROVING YOUR DISCIPLINE

Certainly I don't have all the answers for improving your discipline. However, I do have a number of very cogent, time-tested techniques to help you improve. All of the suggestions will require action and thorough implementation if they are to have a beneficial effect on your results.

1. **Make a Schedule.**
   In order to help you keep your trading signals up to date, set aside a given time of the day or week during which you will do the necessary calculations, charts or other market work. Doing the same work every day of the week will help you get into a specific routine, and this in turn, will eliminate the possibility (or greatly reduce it) of not being prepared when a major move develops.

2. **Don't Try to Do Too Much.**
   Attempt to specialize at one particular trading approach.

If you try to trade into too many markets at one time, or with too many systems at one time, your work will become a burden, you will not look forward to it and you will be more prone to let your studies fall behind. Ideally, seek to work in no more than three to five markets at any given point in time, and attempt to specialize at only one specific system.

3. **Use a Checklist.**
   One of my favorite analogies for the trader to consider is the similarity between the trader and the airplane pilot. Before take-off a good airplane pilot goes through his or her checklist, marking off all of the various items that must be completed or checked prior to take-off. I certainly would not want to fly in plane with a pilot who was sloppy in this procedure—would you?

   The trader who wishes to eliminate trading errors should also maintain such a checklist, consulting it regularly or preferably before each trade is made. Of all of my suggestions the checklist is probably the best one for all traders. I would suggest that even after your checklist has become automatic, you still maintain it, since lack of discipline is likely to attack you at almost any time. It can strike without notice and often does.

4. **Do Not Accept Third-Party Input Once Your Decision Has Been Made.**
   I have come to respect the fact that good traders are usually loners. They must do their work in isolation, and they must implement their decisions in isolation. A pushy or talkative broker, a well-intentioned friend or a very persuasive newsletter can often sway you from a decision that only you should make. There are times when your decision will be wrong, but these are part of the learning experience, and you alone must make your decisions based upon the facts as you see them.

If you have decided to follow your own trading system, then by all means follow it and forget about other input. If, however, your system is based upon deriving input from other sources, then strive to implement your decisions without being swayed from them once your mind has been made up. The benefits of deciding on your own far outweigh the potential benefits of having too much input.

5. **Evaluate Your Progress.**

Feedback is a very important part of the learning process. Keep track of how you are doing with your trading, not only in terms of dollars and cents, but in terms of specific signals, behavior and techniques. This will give you an idea of how closely you are staying with the rules, which rules you are breaking, and how often you may be breaking them.

It is important to know when you make mistakes, but it is more important to know what kind of mistakes you made and how often you made them. This will help you overcome the lack of discipline that causes trading errors to occur.

6. **Learn from Every Loss.**

Losses are tuition. They are expensive and they must be good for something. The something to which I am referring is, of course, learning. Learn from each loss and do your very best to avoid taking the same loss twice or more for the same reason. Do not repeat the same errors. To do so indicates that your discipline is not improving.

7. **Understand Yourself.**

This is certainly a big job and not one easily accomplished. It is extremely important that you understand your motivation and your true reasons for trading the markets. Frequently individuals will do poorly in the markets because their objectives and goals are not well-established.

This issue is discussed in another chapter and I suggest that you refer to the relevant chapter and read my comments. Self-understanding helps clarify your personal goals and thereby makes the process of attaining your goals more specific.

8. **Work with Your Trading System and Remain Dedicated to It.**
   If you are like most traders, you will have done considerable research on a trading method or system. Some traders, however, become quickly disenchanted with their systems and hop from one technique to another. This is one of the worst forms of poor discipline. It does not allow sufficient time for a system to perform. In so doing, the speculator takes considerably more overall risk than he or she should.

9. **Check Your Objectives.**
   At times, poor training discipline can be a function of unclear objectives. If you have decided that you want to trade for the short term only, then you have a very clear objective. However, if you are not certain about the time frame of your trading, about the trading system you plan to use as your vehicle, about the relationship you wish to have with your broker, about the quotation equipment you plan to use (if any), then you will be prone to make mistakes and have poor discipline.

   My suggestion is to make all major trading decisions before you even get started with your trading. Some corrections can be made along the way, but a majority of decisions must be made prior to any serious trading.

10. **Know When to Quit.**
    In order to improve your trading discipline, it is important to have an objective measure of when you will terminate a given trade, profitably or unprofitably. Whether

this is done at a particular price or a particular dollar amount is of no consequence. The fact remains that you must know when you have had enough.

11. **Make Commitments and Keep Them.**
In trading it is important to make and keep commitments in the markets just as it is in every phase of human endeavor and interaction. If, however, you do not make a commitment, or if the commitment you make is not clear, then you stand the chance of not following through on an important phase of your trading. For this reason, I encourage all traders to make specific commitments, not only in terms of such things as trading systems, trading approach, available capital, maximum risk, etc., but also in terms of each and every trade they make.

Do not make the trade unless you are fully committed to it. What does this mean? It means that many individuals are prone to establish a position in the market based on what "looks like" a good signal or when it "looks like the market wants to turn higher." In other words, commitments are made on the basis of vague indications.

In order to make a commitment that will serve you well, do not make commitments that are based upon sketchy information or you know from the start are doomed to failure. The uneasy feeling you get when you make such a decision will be enough to let you know that you are not making a commitment based on correct procedures.

There are many more ways to improve your discipline, but quite a few of these are probably very specific to your individual situation. One good way in which to determine how, where, when and what type of commitment you wish to make is to examine your individual situation by using a checklist or questionnaire designed to ascertain the precise nature of your situation. Ordinarily, only a brief amount of thought and analysis are necessary for each individual to ascertain his or her situation.

SUMMARY

Discipline is the single most important quality a trader can possess, with the possible exception of persistence. Though discipline cannot be taught or learned in a classroom type of setting, there are many things traders can do to facilitate the learning process. This chapter discussed the relevant aspects of discipline and made suggestions regarding how discipline might be improved.

Chapter

8

The Art of
Contrary Thinking

Hundreds of years ago, when the tulip mania was sweeping Holland, no one would have envisioned that many years later, the events of those times would be seen as lessons for the speculator of modern times.

For those of you who are unfamiliar with the tulip mania, suffice to say that it was an event that marked a dark but exemplary period in the psychological and economic history of humankind. The mania which swept Holland can only be described in market terms as panic buying of a commodity that was in great demand, but that had no other value than what people were willing to buy and sell it for. The price of tulip bulbs increased by several thousandfold over a brief period of time, during which frenzied speculation engulfed virtually all of Holland. Overnight, fortunes were made and lost as speculators rushed to buy and sell this "precious commodity."

Today we can only look back in wonderment on those times, shaking our heads and saying, "How could something like this have happened?" Yet, we need not look too far back in our own history to see countless examples of similar manias sweeping our markets. Whether these occurred in the areas of land, real estate, precious metals, sugar or the stock market, is irrelevant. The fact remains that panic and mania are still very much a part of our "modern" society. Emotion still closely governs speculators in all walks of life and in all markets.

In our troubled and volatile times, there is no single market sector as subject to emotional fluctuations as is the futures market. The slightest rumor or news can send the markets skyrocketing or plummeting precipitously with no seeming end in sight, as the frenzy feeds upon itself.

Ultimately, economic reality takes hold and prices eventually return to their proper levels. In the interim, however, emotion and psychological manifestation rule the pits. To understand the psychology of the pit, to understand the psychology of the crowd, to understand the psychology of the speculator and to understand the manner in which these can be best used to your advantage, is to understand the power and the art of contrary opinion.

Although the power of contrary thinking is well-documented and well-understood, it is somewhat unquantifiable, and hence rather elusive in spite of its immense conceptual value. An idea that cannot be quantified is, unfortunately, one that will be difficult to employ in a scientific setting. This is why the concepts advanced by proponents of contrary thinking do not necessarily correspond with the performance of contrary opinion techniques. However, let's first examine precisely what I mean by contrary opinion in order to see how it can be of practical value to the speculator.

WHAT IS IT?

Contrary thinking is the art of thinking and interpreting reality in a different fashion from what the majority of individuals may be doing. Contrary thinking is possible in every form of human endeavor and there are literally millions of individuals who are contrary thinkers as a way of life.

Thought, however, does not necessarily lead to action, and I think we should understand at the outset that *there is a vast difference between contrary thinkers and contrary doers.* More about this later.

Contrary thinkers want to "zig" while everyone else is "zagging." They expect higher prices while most people expect lower prices. They expect lower prices when most people expect higher prices. Contrary thinking is not necessarily a measure of stubbornness, but rather the ability to avoid being caught up in the sentiment in the "crowd."

There are many extremes in the marketplace and it is a matter of recorded fact that some people are swayed by the direction of a major trend and, moreover, that they are strongly influenced by the opinions of others. Therefore, market movement in a particular direction, if strong enough and long enough, tends to arouse public interest. Traders and investors develop tunnel vision. They see only what they have been told to see, or only what they want to see.

The important facts, the ones that will lead to an eventual change in trend, are often ignored. Even when markets begin to change direction those who have been mesmerized into fervently believing that the trend has not ended, will continue to cling desperately to their beliefs. In the meantime, the contrary thinker has suspected all along that the direction of the trend was due to change, and that the opportunity for profit lay just around the corner.

CLASSIC EXAMPLES

There are literally hundreds of classic examples in the economic history of the world to support the theory that a strong consensus of opinion often suggests an eventual opposite price movement. I could probably turn this chapter into several chapters by citing some fairly lengthy, but certainly interesting, examples of contrary opinion in contemporary times. However, my job is not to function as a history teacher; rather it is to familiarize you with valuable concepts that should be added to your trading repertoire. My comments, will, therefore be brief and concise. For specific examples please refer to the reading list and the bibliography at the end of this book.

ALL AROUND US

Contrary thinking is valuable not only in the markets, but also: in everyday life. There have been many fads and financial fallacies in modern times, but the majority of investors and traders have not learned anything about their own emotional makeup in spite of these events.

The writings of the masters clearly underscore the importance of being a contrarian. To act and think contrary to what the crowd is doing and thinking is a valuable personal quality in every walk of life. Yet, it is important that the contrary thoughts and actions be selective. It is important that contrariness be employed at important turning points in our lives and in the markets.

QUANTIFICATION

There have been a number of attempts throughout the history of the markets to quantify various measures of contrary opinion. These have, however, been only sporadically successful. The concept of odd-lot short sales in the stock market is one application of contrary opinion. It is a measure, essentially, of how bearish small investors are at any given point in time. Naturally, one would expect on the basis of contrary opinion that the more bearish small investors are, the more likely prices are to continue rising. Odd-lot short sales are a measure of actual short selling by small investors as an expression of their bullish or bearish sentiment.

The explanation of this phenomenon of course, is very simple. Essentially it says that the small trader cannot afford to sell short a round lot (100 share blocks) of stock. Furthermore, the odd-lotter is felt to be unsophisticated and relatively uninformed. Therefore, a high bearish consensus of action among odd-lot short sellers often indicates that the opposite is about to happen.

Historically, the odd-lot short sales indicator has translated into a very good tool. On occasion, the odd-lot short sellers have been right, but rarely for too long, and rarely for too much of a move. More often than not, they are incorrect at critical turning points in the stock market.

R. E. Hadaday has advanced the notion that contrary opinion in the futures markets can be measured quantitatively by conducting a survey of sentiment among brokers and advisors on a weekly basis. His reporting service, *Market Vane*, reports regularly the percentages of bullish sentiments for each individual futures market. A sample of Hadaday's work is shown in Figure 8–1.

The Hadaday theory is a most interesting one and its concepts are valid, yet there is still the nagging question about its inability to be more precise in timing the market turns. Hadaday has developed a number of techniques for making timing more precise, yet it would seem to me that there must be a better way to employ contrary opinion in the futures markets. My main objection is that most contrary opinion surveys merely reflect opinion and not action. I contend that *there is a large disparity between market opinion and market action.* Whereas a market may rise and opinions may continue to become exceptionally bullish, if these bullish opinions are not backed up by extremely persistent buying by the public, then the opinions are not especially valid. Contrary opinion works because opinions lead to action. If there is only contemplation but no action, then opinions may not be so valid.

The techniques developed by Hadaday and other followers of contrary opinion have great potential in the markets, but they must be backed up by good timing. If you plan to use bullish consensus or contrary opinion indicators, be certain you use them in conjunction with timing indicators such as those described in this book or with other traditional but effective tools.

Essentially, bullish consensus will let you know when the markets have reached a danger zone on the upside, suggesting the

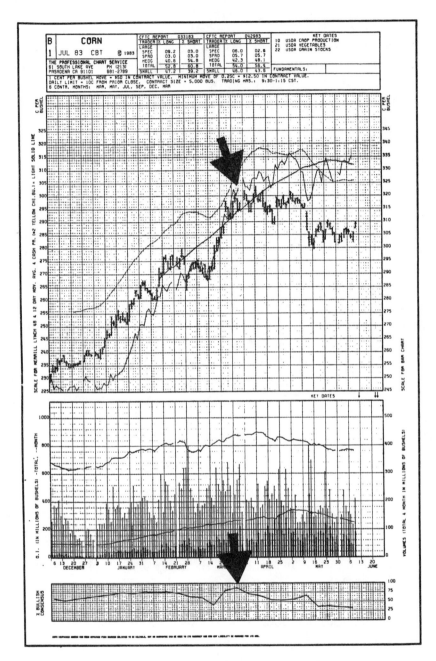

FIGURE 8–1
BULLISH CONSENSUS IN A SPECIFIC FUTURES CONTRACT
(Hadaday, 1983, page C4)
(Reprinted with permission of
Market Vane 61 South Lake Ave #309 Pasadena CA 91101)

possibility of a top or a potential bottom due to exceptionally bearish public and professional sentiment. Figures 8–2, 8–3, and 8–4 illustrate three interesting situations with extreme levels of bullish consensus and timing indicators to suggest a turn in the market. As previously mentioned, the combination of timing and contrary opinion has great potential for all traders. The contrary thinker should always be in touch with levels of bullish or bearish consensus. Though an extreme level on either side does not warrant immediate action, such extremes *do* suggest that a change in trend could occur very soon.

COMMENTS OF TRADERS REPORT

Another way to access the actual bullishness or bearishness of the trader population is by referring to and studying the monthly government *Commitment of Traders Report*. This report contains exceptionally valuable information on the composition of longs and shorts in the marketplace by percentages and groups, showing increases and/or decreases from previous monthly levels. Unfortunately, the report is monthly, and by the time the news is available to most traders it is likely that a change in trend has already taken place. If these figures could be obtained weekly, they would be an invaluable source of information to all speculators.

Martin Weiss and R. Earl Hadaday have collaborated on a publication that gets much closer to the actual state of bullishness or bearishness in the markets by using the data from the *Commitment of Traders Report* to analyze the status of major markets on a monthly basis. The explanation of their work is shown in Figure 8–5. Several illustrations of their concepts translated into practice are illustrated in Figures 8–6, 8–7, and 8–8.

For those who are seriously interested in studying contrary opinion and bullish consensus relationships in the markets, this type of information is essential. As I indicated earlier, it is unfortunate the *Commitment of Traders Report* data is not available more frequently. The individual or organization who can develop a

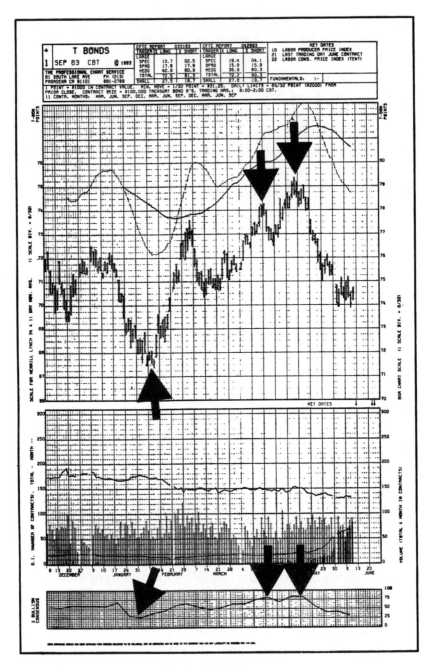

FIGURE 8–2
(Hadaday, 1983, page C25)
(Reprinted with permission of
Market Vane 61 South Lake Ave #309 Pasadena CA 91101)

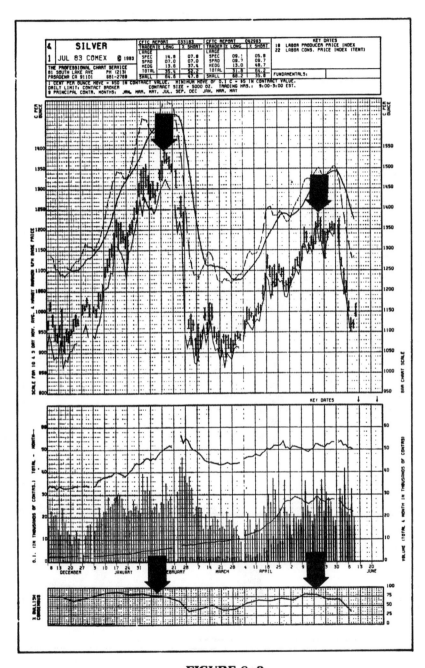

FIGURE 8–3
(Hadaday, 1983, page C22)
(Reprinted with permission of
Market Vane 61 South Lake Ave #309 Pasadena CA 91101)

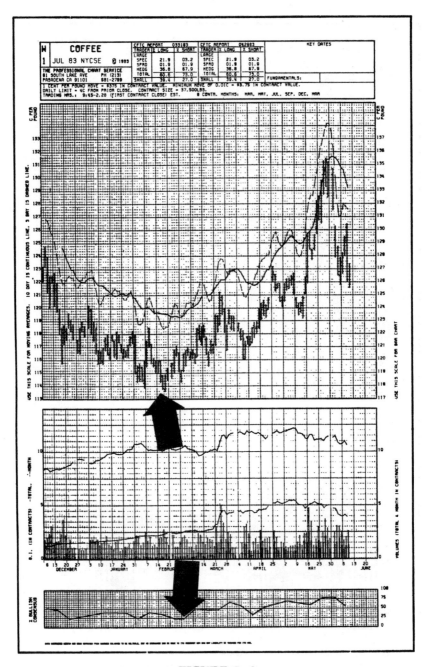

FIGURE 8-4
(Hadaday, 1983, page C16)
(Reprinted with permission of
Market Vane 61 South Lake Ave #309 Pasadena CA 91101)

WOW, an acronym for Who Owns What, is a set of indexes which collectively can give you a clear picture of the activities of the three key groups in the futures market — "commercials," "large speculators," and "small speculators."

The **commercials** are the firms whose business includes the same or similar commodity or financial instruments as those being traded in the futures market. They use the futures market primarily to hedge or protect their positions in the cash market against possible losses.

Speculators, on the other hand, are in the market to make a profit and do not hold positions in the cash market. Among these, large speculators are those whose positions exceed specific levels designated by the Commodity Futures Trading Commission. (In the case of gold, for example, it would be 200 contracts.) Small speculators, by definition, are those whose positions are below these levels.

Typical market composition. Normally — but not always — commercials are net short and speculators are net long, with one group balancing the other. This is because commercials, for whom the futures markets were designed, generally own the physical commodity and must protect or insure themselves against a possible drop in price. Therefore, they sell short in the futures market. They are the real "movers and shakers." The speculators, on the other hand, are typically the buyers of the contracts which the commercials wish to sell. This is because the public generally, but not always, tends to have a bullish orientation towards markets.

The commercials can usually be considered the "insiders" in these markets in that they often have a more intimate knowledge of the existing and future supply/demand relationships for their commodity than does the public. Therefore by watching the degree to which the commercials are hedging in the futures markets we can get a good idea of their outlook on the commodity's price prospects.

The speculator's market position can also be illuminating, allowing us to spot excessive bullishness or unusual bearishness — usually a good sign of a market top or bottom. The relationship between the speculators and commercial market positions is also highly important. When this relationship becomes unbalanced a major move often begins, more often than not favoring the commercials.

In sum, WOW indexes thus serve as a very useful guide to the changing internal structure of the future markets. However, they should be viewed as a complement of — and not as a substitute for — other technical and fundamental methods of analysis.

CHART 1. Prices Chart. This shows the prices for the nearest month covering the most recent 12-month period. Use it to compare the actual market fluctuations with the charts below to help determine why prices have moved up or down, and what might be expected in the future.

CHART 2. Open Interest by Group. The top line shows the total open interest (contracts outstanding). However, this chart goes beyond other charts on open interest by monitoring the open interest of each of the three primary groups. It was designed to tell you three things: (1) which group has been primarily responsible for any rise in total open interest: (2) the relative importance of each group over the most recent 12-month period; and (3) whether each group is expanding or contracting its own market participation.

CHART 3. Bullish Consensus. These figures, the result of a survey of advisors polled each week by Market Vane, attempt to gauge the percentage of market participants who are bullish. Readings above 80% indicate an overbought condition while readings below 20% indicate the market is oversold. The graph shows both weekly readings and a monthly average.

CHART 4. Group Postures. Use this chart in conjunction with Chart 5, the Market Composition pie chart. It is derived by subtracting each primary group's short positions from its long positions, leaving a net figure. For example, if commercials are above the zero line, they are net long. If they are below the zero line, they are net short. This is portrayed over time, showing how these relationships are changing over the most recent 12-month period.

Thus, it is now possible to identify a trend in each of the primary group's movements. For example, let's say that the line representing commercials is below zero, but that it has been rising for the past several months. You would know that, although they are still net short, they have been in the process of covering their shorts. Conversely, suppose the line representing small speculators is above zero, but has been failing. You could further conclude that small speculators have been selling their longs which the commercial interests have been buying.

Now we take this analysis to the bottom line conclusion. If the Monthly Price chart shows prices have been falling during this period, we could safely say that: (1) The speculators who were long are being stopped out; and (2) that these speculators have been selling more than the commercials have wanted to buy — resulting in falling prices.

FIGURE 8-5   EXPLANATION OF "WOW" INDEXES

CHART 5. Market Composition. The total pie represents total open interest (less spreads). It is selected into six sections, each representing the share held (whether long or short) by the three primary groups — commercials, large speculators, and small speculators. Because the total number of short positions always equals the total number of long positions, the left half of the circle showing the shorts will always equal the right half of the circle, the longs.

The purpose of the chart is twofold — first, to allow you to readily perceive the dominance of any particular group in the current time period; and, second, to quickly see to what extent each primary group is either long or short.

CHART 6. Positions of Large Speculators. This chart will show us a total along with its two components — long positions and short positions. For example, the chart in effect tells us (a) if large speculators are entering the market and (b) on which side — long or short. Or, if they are leaving the market, whether they are covering their short positions or liquidating their long positions. (Note: Since the total in this chart is a combination of both short and long positions, it represents two times the actual open interest controlled by this group.)

CHART 7. Positions of Commercials. This presents the same information as Chart 6 but for commercials.

CHART 8. Positions of Small Speculators. This presents the same information as Chart 6 but for small speculators.

TABLE 1. Market Composition Rankings. This table ranks each market according to the share of total open interest controlled by each of the primary groups. It answers the question: Which market is most dominated by a particular group? It can show you which of the three primary groups actually holds the decision-making power in each market. For example, if the table were to show that commercials hold the biggest share of open interest in the gold market, then you should pay particular attention to their actions when you are contemplating a gold trade. In another market, such as lumber, you may find that it is the small speculators who control the largest share, implying that their behavior should be monitored closely. Markets dominated by small speculators tend to be volatile due to the inability of many small speculators to withstand market moves against their positions.

TABLE 2. Market Composition Rankings — Long or Short. This table ranks each market according to the percent of total open interest — long or short — controlled by each of the primary groups. Thus, the percent of open interest figures in Table 1 are broken apart into percent long and percent short, and then ranked separately.

FIGURE 8–5   EXPLANATION OF "WOW" INDEXES (Continued)

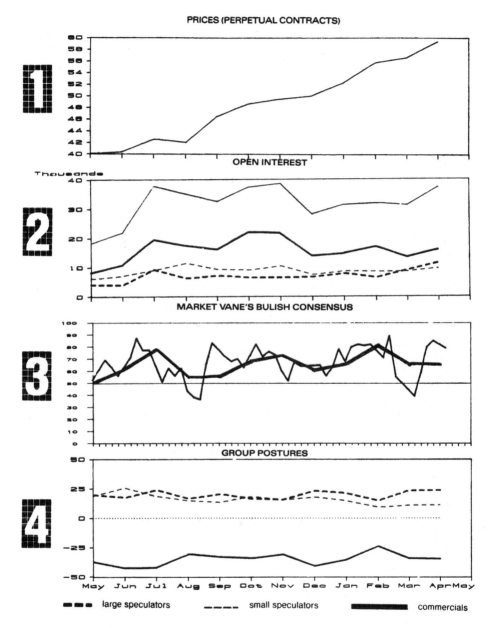

PRICES (PERPETUAL CONTRACTS)

OPEN INTEREST

MARKET VANE'S BULISH CONSENSUS

GROUP POSTURES

large speculators   small speculators   commercials

FIGURE 8–6
Reprinted with permission of Weiss Research
P.O. Box 2923 W. Palm Beach FL 33402 and
Market Vane 61 South Lake, Pasadena CA 91101.

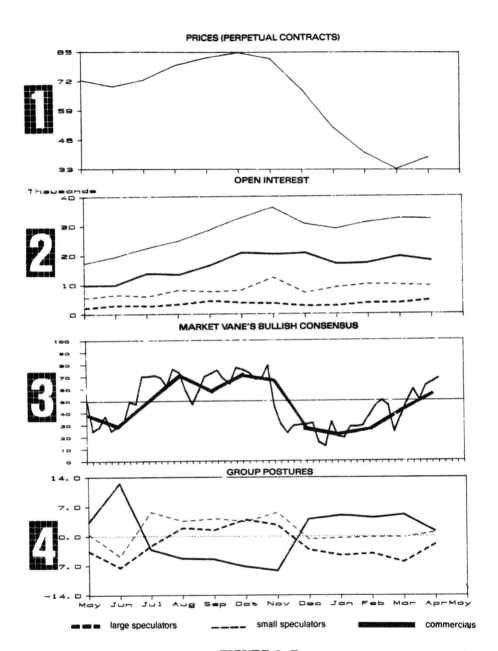

PRICES (PERPETUAL CONTRACTS)

OPEN INTEREST

MARKET VANE'S BULLISH CONSENSUS

GROUP POSTURES

■ ■ ■ large speculators — — — small speculators ▬▬▬ commercials

FIGURE 8–7
Reprinted with permission of Weiss Research
P.O. Box 2923 W. Palm Beach FL 33402 and
Market Vane 61 South Lake, Pasadena CA 91101.

The Art of Contrary Thinking

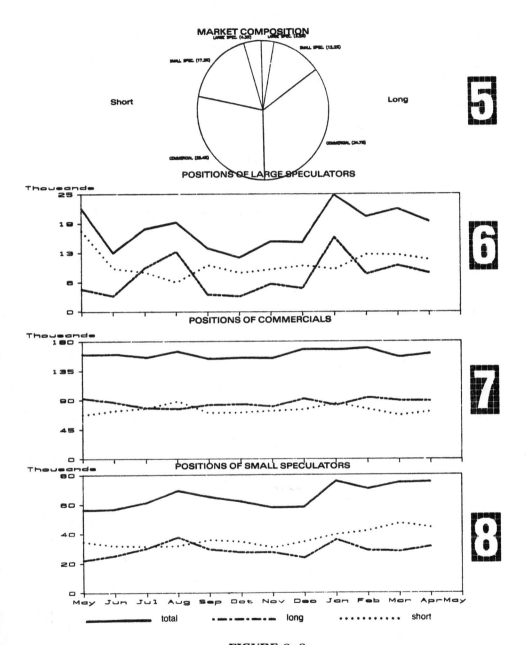

FIGURE 8–8
Reprinted with permission of Weiss Research
P.O. Box 2923 W. Palm Beach FL 33402 and
Market Vane 61 South Lake, Pasadena CA 91101.

a reporting system that studies similar distribution or that arrives at the heart of bullish/bearish consensus in a more specific and, in particular, more frequent fashion, will truly have an exceptionally valuable market tool.

SUMMARY

Contrary opinion is an important market concept. Traders should be aware of bullish and bearish consensus of opinion, taking caution when levels become too high or too low.

Chapter
9

How to Trade
Like a "Pro"

In previous chapters, I've outlined some of the specific methods by which futures and options price trends may be analyzed. As you have seen, they are many and varied. Ultimately, each trader implements a slightly different technique in his or her work, a technique which combines art with science, "gut feel" and instinct with market work and technical analysis. This is why two traders looking at the same information can achieve distinctly different results. This is why the same supposedly mechanical technique will not be seen by all individuals as yielding the same signals and/or indicators. Through my years of trading experience I have seen many traders prosper, yet many more have fallen by the wayside, victimized more by their own inability to trade like a winner than by poor or ineffective trading systems.

My work has shown that futures trading, after all is said and done, is no different than sports, poker, the grocery store business or medicine. True, there are some clear-cut differences. However, there are more similarities than there are differences. Let's take a look at some of the *common traits* shared by most successful individuals, regardless of their specific profession or vocation. Here are some characteristics revealed by my experience and observations.

1. **Discipline** is an absolute necessity. Whether you're running a bar, a bakery, or a futures account, you must know an opportunity when you see it, you must not jump at false opportunities and you must know when to call it quits if an opportunity has turned sour. This all requires self-control, discipline and the ability to act on opportunities that are right for you. Discipline is also required in attending to day-to-day details of your business. If trading is your business, then the day-to-day operations must necessarily include your chart work, calculations, system evaluation signals, bookkeeping, etc. For more details on discipline see Chapter 7.

2. **Persistence** is second on my list, but it ranks as first in importance along with discipline. In every form of business, persistence pays off. Persistence means that one must not allow several losses to dissuade one from action. Naturally, there is a fine line between persistence and bull-headedness. In futures trading it may take quite a few successive losses before a large victory can be scored. This is true in other businesses, as well. Though it is important to know when you've been beaten, it is also important to know when not to quit. Persistence is also vital in finding a trading system and method best suited to your needs.

3. **Patience** is an important quality. It is often necessary to wait for the right opportunity, rather than acting on the wrong opportunities. Since there are many things one can do in the market which are wrong, and only a few which are right, it is very important to be patient in awaiting the right opportunity.

4. **Independence** is right up there with the others. Trading in futures, or for that matter, participation in any form of risk taking for financial gain, is a lonely venture. Many times it is necessary to look the other way, close your eyes and take action contrary to what literally all of those around you are doing. It is often necessary to ignore well-intentioned input from friends, associates and brokers. Trading ideas, trading systems and implementation of trades are all difficult because they involve singleness of purpose and firm resolution to do what you believe to be right. The influence of outside forces and factors can frequently be destructive and dissuasive. Therefore, it is necessary for the successful trader to do "his or her own thing" with a minimum of external influence, particularly from those with supposedly good intentions.

5. **Contrary thinking** is, perhaps, the greatest single psychological quality a trader can possess. If contrary thinking is not one of your traits, you must work toward developing it. The ability to examine the consensus of opinion, and the more significant ability to trade *contrary to the consensus of opinion* are very important factors contributing to trader success. This is true since a majority of traders are wrong a majority of the time. Therefore, if you find yourself in strong agreement with most other traders, the chances are quite good that you are wrong.

   However, if you find yourself at odds with a good majority of traders most of the time, and if you act on these contrary opinions (which will usually be confirmed by your trading system), you will find that you are likely to reap handsome profits. Contrary thinking helps you avoid being trapped by the panic and fear of the crowd. It allows you to step in when the worst or best are about over, taking appropriate positions accordingly.

6. **The ability to act quickly,** though last on my list of the top six qualities, is by no means last in importance. Many individuals are frozen by fear or indecision when the time to act arrives. Their trading system is good, their decisions are correct, yet their inability to act is a destructive quality.

As you've seen in previous chapters, the futures markets are fast. They do not wait. In futures trading it is not enough just to be "in the right place at the right time," you must also *act*. There are ways in which this skill can be developed. Suffice it to say, however, that if you do not possess this quality now, you will need to do some major reconstruction of your personality.

To impress upon you the importance of how quickly the futures markets move, examine Figure 9–1. This figure shows December silver futures prices on a 15-minute bar chart of the high, low, open and close during the period 10/19/84 through 10/26/84. Examine very carefully the behavior of prices on 10/25. Note that during this particular day the price of December silver futures moved from a low of 731 up to a daily high of 755 (a move of $1,700 per contract) during a period of 75 minutes! Then prices dropped from the 765 high to a daily low of 730 in 3½ hours, only to run up again by 10¢ ($500 per contract) in 30 minutes. An examination of the price every five minutes (Figure 9–2) shows that the large move actually happened over a period of 10 minutes.

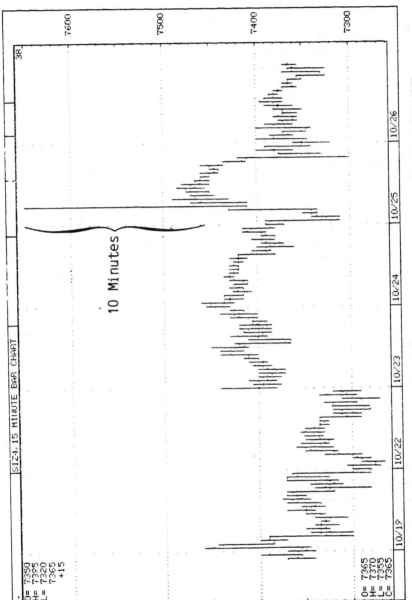

FIGURE 9–1 FIFTEEN-MINUTE DECEMBER SILVER FUTURES CHART SHOWING LARGE INTRADAY MOVE IN PRICE
(Reprinted with Permission of Commodity Quote Graphics)

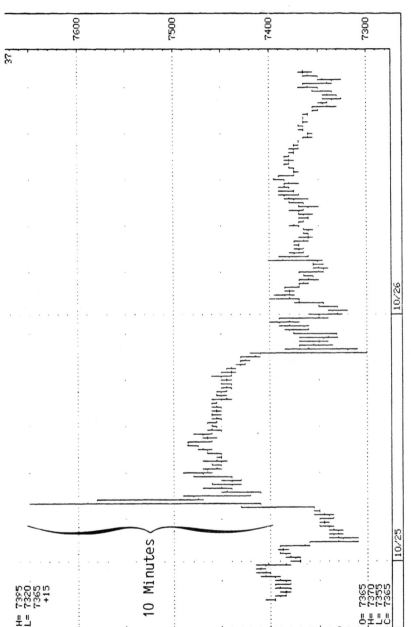

**FIGURE 9–2 FIVE-MINUTE CHART SHOWING CLOSE UP OF
SILVER PRICE MOVEMENT IN FIGURE 9–1
(Reprinted with Permission of Commodity Quote Graphics)**

Though these moves have been intentionally selected to make a point, they are *not uncommon.* The futures trader who hesitates has lost a vital opportunity to make a high percentage on invested money. In this case, for example, assume that it took the trader five minutes to decide that he should follow his signal to buy silver. Assume it took him another two minutes to have his buy order executed. It is now eight minutes into a 10-minute move. Had the trader been buying at the market, he would have bought at or close to the top, eventually ending up with a *loss rather than a profit.*

WHY ARE THERE SO MANY LOSERS?

As you can plainly see, the qualities required for success in futures trading are just as important as, if not more important than, the system one decides to use. The analogy I like to use in discussing the trader and the system is that of the car and the driver. In order to win a race, you may spend millions on perfecting the ultimate vehicle. Yet, if you have a poor driver, or one who cannot effectively manipulate the powerful vehicle through competition, traffic, danger and adverse weather, you will not win the race and your investment in the ultimate vehicle will be a total waste. This is why there are so many losers in the futures market, or, for that matter, in every form of investment.

Taking the car-and-driver analogy one step further, you can see that a good driver in an average vehicle can actually win the race. Car and driver are inseparable just as system and trader are. Like it or not, there is a strong and persistent interaction of the two. You cannot have one without the other. I maintain, therefore, that in the investment and speculation worlds, too much attention has been given to the *car* and very little attention has been given to the *driver.*

The world is full of investors and traders who, were it not for their losing personalities and trading habits, could be very successful. I have found that *the system* is not nearly as important as *the trader.* In answer to the question, "Why are there so many losers?" I say simply that they have not *learned to be winners.* Some winners are born; most winners are created.

HOW TO KNOW IF YOU'RE A LOSER
BEFORE YOU BECOME ONE

At the risk of offending my audience, I will say that if you're a loser you already know it. If you don't know it, take a bit of time to examine some of the traits I've outlined in Figure 9–3.

Let's face it, the greatest part of starting on the road to success is getting off the road to failure. Getting off the road to failure requires you to first recognize what road you're on. The car-and-driver analogy is applicable here, as well. If you're driving from point *A* to point *B* and you get lost, you may eventually find your way through luck, but this is unlikely. The only effective and prompt way to find the proper direction (before you run out of gas) is by asking someone who knows and then *following the directions.*

It is also true in futures trading. The checklist, if answered honestly, will help you admit to problems you may now have. In recognizing them, half the battle will have been won.

1. I have trouble getting and staying organized.
2. I cannot afford to lose too much money in futures trading.
3. I have been accused of acting on impulse.
4. I have limited time to work on the markets.
5. Generally speaking, I've had poor interpersonal relationships most of my adult life.
6. I have never used a trading system in my work with stocks or futures.
7. I've been told that I give up too easily.
8. I like to act with the majority since it makes me comfortable.
9. I feel good when my broker agrees with my trading decisions.
10. Success in futures trading and investing is mostly a matter of good luck.
11. Most of my business ventures have met with failure.
12. In order to win at futures I need a trading system better than most.
13. I tend to get frustrated quickly.
14. Many times I get frozen by indecision.
15. I tend to make poor decisions under pressure.

FIGURE 9–3 CHECKLIST OF LOSING MARKET BEHAVIORS

Though by no means exhaustive, the listing in Figure 9–3 will act as a very quick screening test for success. I have found that if 85 percent or more of your answers to the questions above are "yes," then you need to do much work on yourself *before* you can begin trading. The greatest thing this book can do for you, above and beyond the simple mechanics of trading, is to let you know whether or not you are ready to trade.

Regardless of how good you may think you will be, the acid test of trading always creates pressures that you have not previously experienced. Preparation, planning, personality change and perseverance are the "4 Ps" of trading that must be learned by all who seek success in futures, or for that matter, in any business venture.

HOW TO THINK AND ACT LIKE A PRO

Now that you've been honest with yourself, now that you've confessed to some of your shortcomings in life and in the marketplace, we can begin some preliminary work on how to improve and how to trade like a professional. Let me say for starters that I am assuming you have a system that's correct at least 60 percent of the time. Here are a few things you can do *now* in order to improve on your eventual trading success.

Get Organized

Organization is vital to the success of any venture, since it is important to know where you are headed, when you expect to get there and the vehicles you will use to reach your destination. Without organization these tools can often be misplaced. Your charts, books, formulae, trading rules, telephone numbers, etc., must be readily available. The present brief paragraph is meant merely to guide you to one area which will help you trade like a professional.

Develop Discipline

This is, of course easier said than done. There are many ways in which it can be achieved. One of them is to take a course on self-improvement such as those offered by the Dale Carnegie Institute. You will learn that success requires discipline and that discipline can be learned. Discipline can often be improved through the simple application of behavioral learning techniques. My book, *The Investor's Quotient* (New York: John Wiley & Sons, 1980) gives specific suggestions and techniques designed to help you improve your discipline. In addition, there are many simple exercises you can use.

Remember that discipline from one area of your life tends to be reflected in all others. Therefore, if you lack self- discipline when it comes to changing such negative habits as over-drinking, over-weight and overeating, and smoking, then you will probably lack the discipline required for successful trading. You may need to conquer these habits first, or you may need to conquer all lack of discipline at once.

Finally, remember that discipline is not synonymous with rigidity. Being rigid in following rules is not necessarily a form of discipline. Being a disciplined trader also means being flexible enough to change course as soon as you see that the action you have taken is not working. The rigid trader will believe too strongly in his or her trading rules and this can prove destructive. Trading is a game of probability and there is *no room for rigidity when it comes to probability.* See Chapter 19 for specifics.

Develop a Trading Approach You Can Truly Use— Don't Get Too Sophisticated

One of the greatest limitations on success in trading is that systems become too complicated, too burdensome, or too time-consuming to use. If you build a boat, make certain you can get your boat into the water. Once in the water, make certain you can move.

Too many traders spend too much time developing complicated, "sophisticated" trading systems that are too difficult to implement. My knowledge of top-ranking, successful futures traders shows that *most of them use simple methods.* You will hear this repeated again and again.

"Keep it simple" is one of the foremost rules. If you keep it simple you will have less trouble with self-discipline and you will shorten your market response time. This alone will prove very valuable. Therefore, *keep it simple!* See Chapters 9, 18, and 19 for details.

Keep Impulsive Trading to a Minimum—
Stay Relatively Isolated

There's a great deal to be said for isolationism in trading. In order to keep free of impulse, it is often best to *not know the news.* Therefore you "can keep your head while all those around you are losing theirs." You will, in so doing, avoid the costly errors that are so often the result of impulse rather than system.

I favor *isolation.* I prefer *not* to listen to the radio or television news, *not* to read the newspapers, *not* to listen to the opinions of others, and *not* to discuss the markets, even with other professionals. I do this because I know that I may have weaknesses. In order to be strong and avoid impulsive actions motivated by the emotions of fear and/or greed I must limit the amount of extraneous informational input.

Plan Your Trades and Trade Your Plans

This market cliché is just as true today as when it was coined. It is the best way to avoid virtually all of the losing inputs. If you are prepared, and if you act according to your plan, you will have taken the first and most important step to conquering lack of self-discipline.

Keep Your Objectives Clearly in Mind

Chapter 18 discusses trading objectives. You must always keep your goals in mind. If you are a short-term trader, then you must think and act like one. However, if you're a long-term trader, then your perception of the markets and your corresponding actions must be consistent with these objectives. I have found it best to have a list of objectives and goals handy for quick reference during times of need.

Deal Effectively with Stress—Vent Frustrations—Don't "Live the Market"

In order to improve market decisions, it is necessary to deal effectively with stress. There are many ways in which this can be done. Exercise is one good way to cope with stress. It will help you vent frustrations and it will give you a good chance to get your mind off the markets. Furthermore, *leave the markets at the office.* If you plan to trade as your profession, then this rule is vital. If you plan to trade in your spare time, then have certain hours set aside for this activity and do not become a market addict.

Keep Commission Costs Low

The overhead of trading consists of losses and commissions. Commissions comprise a built-in loss factor. Poor order execution comprises another aspect of the built-in cost of doing business. Between poor order fills and commissions, about 25 percent of profits can be eaten up before your very eyes.

Many traders are shocked when they see how much they've paid out in commissions every year. Some traders who want and need the advice of brokers will need to do business with a "full-service house." They will, therefore, pay higher commissions.

There's nothing wrong with this provided it is cost-effective. Just because you deal with a full-service house and pay higher commissions doesn't mean you will fail.

However, *you must get some return for what you are paying in higher costs.* If you do not get a return, then you're not making a sound business decision. If you trade frequently without needing advice or information, then you are entitled to lower commissions. You can ask your full-service broker for a discount. Be informed about their discount policies. Don't be afraid to ask how much trading you will need to do in order to benefit from the commission break.

Finally, if you see that you are not using any of the information put out by the house you're dealing with, take the time to investigate a switch to discount commissions with another house. But first, inquire with your current broker if he can lower his rates since a *good relationship with your broker is very important.* Chapter 12 covers these issues in detail.

Avoid Over-Trading—Be Conservative

One of the greatest secrets to success in trading is to avoid "over-trading." This mistake is caused by the erroneous assumption that you must be in every market at all times. There is no substance or truth to this belief. As a matter of fact, market professionals like to concentrate on certain markets and only on certain types of moves.

You cannot and should not be in all markets at all times. Therefore, be conservative and trade only the best signals with the most reasonable risk-to-reward ratios. This is discussed in various chapters throughout the book.

SUMMARY

In order to be successful in the futures markets, there are many behaviors you will need to cultivate and others you will need to eliminate. This chapter provided a checklist designed to help you evaluate yourself, and it made suggestions for changing some of the behaviors and attitudes you now have that may prevent successful trading and speculation in futures and options.

Chapter
10

Twenty-One Tools
for Successful
Trading

The student of futures trading has a very clear and concise goal. *This goal is not primarily to beat the market or to become skillful for the sake of skill alone.* The true speculator is, first and foremost, *interested in profits and success.*

As you can tell from your own experience, from other aspects of life, and from my many caveats in this book, there is no sure-fire simple road to success in the markets. With so many techniques to choose from, with so many different orientations, and with so many trading systems available to speculators, what you ultimately develop will be an individual approach tailor-made (by yourself) to suit your purposes. Whether what you end up with is a purely mechanical approach based upon the research of others, or a primarily subjective approach based upon your own interpretations and studies, the fact remains that the ultimate decision-making task is yours and yours alone.

Yet, regardless of what you select or how you select it, you can readily see from what you have already read in this book, and from what you may already know, that there are some general similarities and common threads that interweave every approach to futures trading. These commonalities influence and regulate the success or failure of virtually every trader.

While it may very well be true that some individuals can and do achieve success by breaking all the rules, it is also true that such individuals are clearly in the minority and that their success is the exception rather than the rule. Unless you are an individual blessed with fantastic luck, you will need to achieve success in the futures markets the good old fashioned way, you'll have to earn it. The only way to earn lasting success is through the diligent and disciplined application of specific techniques and methods, few of which are directly related to systems, and most of which are clearly the function of attitudes, psychology, and discipline.

You may not want to hear this, but the fact is that it matters little what system or systems you select, how tremendous their hypothetical performance may be or how well others may have done with these systems. What ultimately matters, as you very well know, is how you apply the systems, and the consistency with which you can put the techniques into operation.

Understandably, the human being is not a computer, and he or she cannot achieve the same level of perfection that may be required to institute a trading system in complete accordance with the ideal conditions under which it was tested. The degree of slippage, drawdown and trader error is often significant. Furthermore, it frequently seems that real-time market conditions deteriorate the performance of most systems and, in fact, no system based on hypothetical, or computer-simulated or -tested results can be taken as worthwhile unless these results can be replicated with reasonable similarity in the markets themselves.

It is for these reasons, among others, that the steps toward trading success do not rest exclusively, or for that matter heavily, upon selection of a trading system. Though I know that the selection of a system is important, I suspect that its value has been overstated, particularly by those with a vested interest in selling systems or in managing a fund based on such systems. In order to achieve success it will be necessary for you to follow most, if not all, of the time-tested rules of profitable trading.

Though I will begin my "List of Twenty-One" with items related to system selection, you will observe that these items do not dominate the list. Remember also that variations on each item in the list are certainly possible in order to adapt them to your particular situation.

TWENTY-ONE TOOLS TO BETTER TRADING

1. **Find or develop a trading system** that has a real-time record (or computer-tested record) of 70 percent or more winning trades, with a ratio of approximately 2 to 1 in terms of dollars made versus dollars lost per trade (including commissions as losses). In the absence of real-time results, computer results are acceptable, provided you have made provisions for the limitations as discussed earlier in this book. Though the figures just given need not be replicated exactly, attempt to get close.

2. **The system you find or develop should be consistent with your time limitations** or availability (with or without a computer system). If the signals are generated by an advisory service, then make certain you have familiarized yourself with the basics of the system, its trading approach and other details of the system as described earlier in the text.

3. **Select a brokerage firm** that will be compatible with your needs. If you are an independent trader wishing no input whatsoever, then select a discount firm that gives good service and prompt order executions. If, however, you are a novice trader requiring a full-service firm, then be willing to pay higher commissions in order to have your needs fulfilled.

4. **Select a broker within the firm, or specify your needs to the firm** if you will not be working with one particular broker. Make certain that both you and the broker are aware of each others' needs, and keep the lines of communication clear.

5. **Make certain you have sufficient risk capital** to trade the system you have selected. Be certain that your risk capital is truly risk capital and not funds upon which you are otherwise counting on for some future purpose.

6. **Develop and formulate your trading philosophy.** As you know, your perceptions of trading, your expectations, your goals and your market orientation (*i.e.*, long-term, short-term, etc.) are all factors that contribute either to success or to failure.

7. **Plan your trades and follow through on your plans.** Attempt not to trade on whim. Rather, work from a trading plan each and every day so you will avoid the temptation of making spur-of-the-moment decisions that are not based on any system or method you are using.

8. **Be an isolationist.** There is great value in being an isolationist when it comes to speculation. You don't necessarily want anyone else's input. You don't necessarily want anyone else's opinions. As time goes on, as the lessons you learn begin to accumulate, you will realize that your own good opinion is just as valuable, perhaps more so, than the opinions of any others, experts or novice.

9. **Make a commitment; take the plunge!** Make a commitment to trading. The commitment should consist of rules, organizational procedures, goals and expectations. Delineate these carefully, with consideration and with forethought. By making your plans, you will avoid costly errors that are not consistent with your plans.

10. **Once you've decided—act!** Don't hesitate one moment once your trading decisions have been made (whether the decision is to get into a trade or to get out of a trade). It matters not whether you are taking a profit or closing out a loss. As soon as you have a clear cut signal to act, don't hesitate. Act as soon as your system says you must act—

no sooner, no later.

11. **Limit risk and preserve capital.** The best way to limit risk is to trade only in 3–6 markets at once and to avoid trading markets that have swings much too large for your account size. Once you have decided to limit risk to a certain dollar amount or to limit risk using a specific technique, make certain you take your losses as soon as they should be taken. Do this on time—not too soon, not too late!

12. **Don't anticipate.** Many traders go astray when they anticipate signals from their trading system. The trading system is your traffic light. The traffic is always heavy. Stop on the red, go on the green, be cautious on yellow. If you anticipate trading signals from your system, you might as well not have a system at all.

13. **The market is the master, you are the slave.** Like it or not, you cannot tell the market what to do. It will always do what it wants and it is your job to figure out what it is doing. Once done, you must follow the market through its many twists and turns. If it is zigging and zagging, then you must zig and zag. If it is trending higher, you must trade from the long side. If it is trending lower, you must trade from the short side.

    It may be instructive for you to review, from time to time, which side of the market most of your trades were on. If you find that you have been bucking the trend of the market, then you must review either your system or your discipline. One of the two (perhaps both) are not functioning properly. Many traders have gone astray by failing to follow the market, thinking that it is their job to forecast the market. The job of the trader is *to follow, not to forecast.* Let's leave forecasting to economists.

14. **Do your homework.** Whether you are using a computer, whether you are a novice or a seasoned veteran, you must keep your research current. Futures markets move so fast

that there is precious little time to update your trading signals once a move has occurred. You must be there at the very inception of a move or shortly thereafter. Otherwise you will have difficulty getting aboard for the bigger move. The only way to do this is to keep your homework up to date. If you have a computer it may be easier. You can program your computer so it will automatically update your signals or system every day at a certain time. Regardless, discipline is always involved and you must keep current.

15. **Avoid emotion.** It is paradoxical that the greatest friend of the speculator is the emotion of others, yet emotion within the speculator is one of his or her greatest enemies. When trading, emotions must be under control and they must be ignored. Regardless of the trend of emotions, their consequences can be exceptionally dangerous to the speculator since they can result in unwarranted actions. I have commented on this previously throughout the book.

16. **Don't take tips, "sure things," or inside information.** The temptation in all of us is to find the easy way. You know that the easy way is rarely the best way. There will always be lottery winners, but your odds of winning any lottery are slim, indeed. Therefore, avoid the temptation of taking tips, following inside information, listening to the opinions of other traders or believing that the person you are listening to or talking to knows more than you do. Sometimes they do, but most of the time they don't. Collective opinions are, of course, helpful in the case of contrary opinion studies, but individual opinions or tips are basically useless to the trader.

17. **When you make money, take some of it away from the market.** When you have been doing well, remember to systematically remove money from your account. Whether you do this on a profitable trade basis or on a time basis

(*i.e.,* daily, weekly, monthly) is not important. *What is important is to do it.*

Traders have winning and losing periods. During the winning times, profits will accumulate rapidly and before you know it you may become impressed with your own success. You will examine ways to expand your trading in view of your tremendous profits. You will look at how much money there is in your account and you will be tempted to trade larger positions.

While there will be a time for this, it is usually not right to do so when you are feeling exceptionally euphoric about your performance. One way to reduce euphoria and put profits away for a rainy day is by having a systematic method of withdrawing profits.

18. **Develop winning attitudes and behaviors.** You can do this by reading the writings of the great traders. Spend more time developing yourself than you do developing your systems. The key variable in the trading success equation is the trader and *not the system.* I maintain that a good trader can make virtually any system work.

19. **"The trend is your friend."** This old expression is known to all, but used by few. Whether you allow the major trend to filter signals from your system as the final deciding factor, or whether you use a system that is based entirely upon trend following principles, always be cautious when your trades are not consistent with the existing trend. Naturally, there will be times when your signals are against the trend. There will be times when the trend is apt to change. However, you should always be careful about trades and signals against the trend since they will most often be wrong.

20. **Don't try to trade too many markets.** There are many different markets, but most move together. There are only a few major market groups. Take one market from each

group, preferably the most active, and focus on it. Few traders can be involved in all markets at once.

21. **Don't lose sight of your goals.** Your goal in futures trading is to make money. There is no goal greater than this in futures trading. Though there may be other benefits such as self-satisfaction, the thrill of trading and the sublimation of hostility and competitive instincts, these are all secondary. If you seek revenge against the market or other traders; if you wish merely to compete for the sake of competition or to trade only for the thrill of trading, then the primary goal of speculation will be lost and so will your money!

SUMMARY

The rules presented in this chapter are based upon my many experiences and observations in futures trading since 1968. Though some rules may be more important to you than others, I know that at one time or another, all of these will be important to all traders. The best way to employ these rules in your trading program is to study them, to keep them at your disposal and to review them regularly. They will help keep you on the right track and they will help keep you honest with yourself.

Perhaps one of the greatest errors a speculator can commit is self-deception. The markets are brutal and the pain of losses is omnipresent. No trader or speculator is immune to losses. I might even go so far as to say that what ultimately separates the winners from the losers is the ability to be honest with oneself. From this rare quality arises clear perception. From a clear perception of reality emanates the ability to use only what is effective and to discard all that is not.

Part 3

The Mechanics
of Trading

Chapter

11

What You Need to Know about Market Information Services

There are many services available to the futures trader ranging from newsletters to chart services. There are positive aspects of some services, but there are some negative attributes, as well. Without citing specific services by name, this chapter seeks to achieve the following goals:

1. To familiarize you with the types of services available,
2. To describe different features of the various services,
3. To help you understand what to look for in a service, and
4. To give you some ideas that may help you save time and money.

WHY USE A SERVICE?

The first and foremost consideration in purchasing any type of service connected with futures trading is its ability to help save you time. If you can purchase a service for several hundred dollars a year which, in the long run, will save you considerable effort and time and even help you make money, then you are practicing good business sense by "farming out" the work to someone else. Today there are many active markets, with many different contract

months, futures options, etc. The individual speculator can purchase considerable market information on a regular basis at a
reasonable cost, thereby avoiding the time, expense and effort
involved in producing the information manually or with one's own
computer system.

It should be remembered that many times the speculator may
wish to do his or her own homework, since this is frequently a
very good way to keep in touch with the markets. In particular,
individuals whose main method of trading is charting should spend
at least their early months of trading doing their own charts, since
much will be learned from observing how the basic chart patterns
develop. These basic understandings and skills may be necessary
at some point in the understanding and application of higher level
concepts.

This is why I strongly recommend that each speculator spend
some time manually calculating (if possible) some of his or her indicators. I myself have had many insights about the market while
manually computing indicators and signals. For the chartist, the
benefits of a service may be enhanced after an initial period of
manual updates.

TYPES OF SERVICES

I categorize futures services in two basic groups, *(a)* those that
provide strictly factual information (i.e., charts and statistics), and
(b) those that provide interpretive market information. It is interesting to note that many services that do not consider themselves
interpretive in nature are, in fact, just that. Of further interest
is the fact that the Commodity Futures Trading Commission and
the National Futures Association, both futures regulatory agencies, require advisory services to be registered in order to dis-
seminate their information. However, many services that are, in
fact, advisory in nature are not required to register as advisors.

INFORMATION SERVICES

There are essentially three types of informational services. They are:

1. Purely statistical services (fundamental and technical),
2. Chart services, and
3. News services.

1. **Statistical Services**

Essentially, statistical services do nothing but report statistics. The statistics may be technical or fundamental, but the key element here is that they do not offer any interpretation of the statistics; they merely report them as they have occurred. In this category, I would include both fundamentally and technically oriented statistical services.

Statistical services may include such things as government reports, government statistics, Commitment of Traders Reports, shipping information, crop reports, planting intentions, etc. Any report that provides merely factual information is considered informational and not interpretative. One should be aware that many services that provide such data also offer their own interpretation of the data. This kind of service I consider to be somewhat advisory in nature, depending upon the fashion in which the information has been reported.

2. **Chart Services**

The area of chart services covers a wide variety of publications. There is, however, a very clear distinction between chart services that merely report factual information, and chart services that interpret and advise based on the chart information. The distinction is important, since the independent futures trader does not wish to clutter his or her mind with opinions or analyses prepared by others. This is very important (as you will recall) to the truly independent trader.

It is interesting to note that some services that in the past were purely informational, have slowly become more advisory oriented. However, they still separate their chart analyses physically from their charts. This is helpful to the independent trader who can simply separate the recommendations and opinions from the charts and dispose of the recommendations in order to avoid being influenced by them.

Ideally, however, I would recommend that the trader who wishes to make his or her decisions totally uninfluenced by the input of other analysts subscribe to a chart service that is purely informational, containing no chart analyses whatsoever.

An interesting sidelight of chart services has developed in recent years. It is becoming more fashionable for chart services to also include various market indicators in chart form along with the charts. These indicators may be helpful to some traders. However, as is the case of market opinions, I find that they are best avoided by the truly independent speculator. As you can well imagine, indicators of such a nature can influence you in both a subtle and overt fashion.

Please understand that I am not judging these indicators useless, nor do I advise all traders to avoid them. I am, however, alerting you to the fact that many traders may not wish to have such input unless they feel they need the additional information, or they are interested in supplementing their market analyses with the input provided by indicators that they feel have good potential.

Other considerations in subscribing to a chart service are equally as important. Perhaps the single greatest feature of any chart service is the user's ability to update his or her charts manually. The chart service should allow sufficient room to project cycles and trendlines into the future, as well as room on which to update the charts. The price scales should be easy to work with, and the paper should be thick enough to allow manual updates. Within reasonable limits, the larger the charts, the better.

An important consideration that many traders have overlooked is the availability of opening prices on a daily price chart. As I have demonstrated elsewhere in this book, opening prices are important to the speculator, perhaps more important than many analysts believe them to be. My preference is for a chart service containing opening prices. Unfortunately, in today's chart service market, this narrows the available choices quite significantly, since most services do not plot opening prices. Certainly, the use of opening prices is a matter of individual preference, but I suggest you give it strong consideration after reviewing some of my work and techniques using opening prices.

3. **News Services**

In some respects, news services are similar to chart services. There are those that report the news and those that report and interpret the news. The *caveats* in this case are similar to those I outlined earlier for the two different types of chart services. Again, an independent trader must evaluate the relevance of the information based on his or her specific needs. Many traders, in fact, prefer not to know the news since their approach is primarily technical. However, for those who do wish to know the news, any interpretation of the news may not be consistent with their modus operandi.

ADVISORY SERVICES

Before digging deeply into the subject of advisory services, let's remember the basic distinction between the two types of traders I have discussed. Certainly, there are individuals who will not be aligned on either extreme, although, as I have stated earlier, it is my opinion in futures trading one would rather be on an extreme than in the middle. The real issue is and will remain, *do you want or do you need an advisory service?* You are the only individual who can answer this question best, but in so doing, you must remember that there are assets and liabilities regardless of which decision you may make.

The benefits of having an advisory service provide its input for your decision are essentially threefold. *(a)* Many advisory services do full-time work on indicators and techniques that may be consistent with your orientation to the market. Consequently, you may save yourself considerable time by subscribing. *(b)* Many advisory services have good performance records that can help you profit in the markets. The other side of the coin is, of course, that all services have their good times as well as bad, just as traders do. *(c)* Advisory services may be valuable in helping your discipline. It is easier for some traders to follow the advice of another than it is for them to take their own good advice. All three points should be considered when making your decision.

On the other hand, there are a number of points to consider on the negative side of advisory services.

1. **Dependency**

   Many traders do not look favorably upon the possibility of becoming dependent on an advisory service. Though the particular advisor or newsletter may be doing well at present, performance could change markedly over time. This is, of course, the risk one takes in depending upon someone else's advice.

2. **Lack of Teaching**

   The individual who subscribes to a service that does nothing more than make recommendations, providing minimal analyses or justification for these recommendations, may find him- or herself not learning anything from the service. Individuals who are in the futures markets in order to further their understanding, and who plan at some point to develop an independent approach, will not benefit from such services.

3. **Results**

It can be difficult to duplicate the results of some advisory services. This could be due to a number of factors including trader discipline or inaccurate/misrepresented reporting of results. Before considering an advisory service, verify performance claims through an independent evaluating service (if one is available for the service you are considering).

4. **Methodological Considerations**

In deciding to commit to a given advisory service or services, it is also important to carefully consider the systems or methods they plan to employ in their trading. In some cases, the methodology of the services is known and clearly stated for potential and current subscribers. In other instances, however, the service may wish to keep strictly confidential most aspects of their approach, giving nothing but buy/sell/hold advice.

There is nothing wrong with either procedure. However, the secretive approach may not satisfy some individuals who feel that they must know why they are committing their money. Furthermore, the secretive approach does not provide any educational benefits to the subscriber. You would do well to take into careful consideration and analysis the approach of any service whose work you are attempting to use as part of your educational advancement in futures trading. Although a number of services provide very general rationale for each of their trading recommendations, the explanations provided are still insufficient to provide any meaningful subscriber education.

EVALUATING A SERVICE

With so many services available to today's commodity trader, I would recommend you follow a number of specific steps and procedures before selecting a service. If you plan to use the service as an alternative to your own futures research or as an adjunct to the work you are already doing, be especially selective. Understand that, although I have a vested interest since I publish several advisory services for speculators, I am attempting to give you a totally unbiased point of view since the topic is a very important one.

Before outlining a step-by-step procedure for you, you must remember that the basic question, which only you can answer, is, "Do you really want to subscribe to an advisory service?" The answer is strictly an individual response that must take into consideration your own needs, assets, strengths and weaknesses. Please remember that my purpose is to provide you with a truthful answer, and not one that will serve my purposes. I am certain that I speak for a majority of trading advisors who publish newsletters when I say that we do not want to entice subscribers to our service unless they can truly employ it either as part of their own research or trade exclusively with our recommendations.

The ultimate goal is for everyone to profit; subscribers and newsletter writers alike. None of us want unhappy subscribers who do not feel that what they have purchased is to their benefit. This is why I would rather discourage someone at the start, as opposed to enticing individuals who are really not ready for an advisory service.

Given the fact that many individuals want to trade futures, but are limited in the time they can devote to a futures analysis, the need arises for an advisory-type service. Individuals who cannot make the time commitment are, therefore, drawn to services that are akin to their market orientations. Those who follow cycles, for example, may be attracted to one type of service, whereas individuals who are more interested in fundamentals may be attracted to a different type of advisory service. It's all a matter of individual preference. There is a market advisory service available for virtually every type of market orientation covering everything from fundamentals to astrologically based systems.

With this background in mind, and with the full realization that advisory services *are not for all speculators*, here are a number of points to consider in selecting a service.

1. **Specificity**
   Some advisory services claim fantastic performance records that, upon closer examination, are discovered to be based on very general recommendations, and leaving too much of the decision-making process to the reader. Vague recommendations can be interpreted in many different ways and, ultimately, the individual making these recommendations can make virtually any claim with 20/20 hindsight. Therefore, when considering a service make certain that its recommendations are specific regarding entry, exit and follow-up. Such specificity can be in the form of specific price orders or in specific market instructions (i.e., buy on Monday's open).

2. **Timeliness**
   Some advisory services are not sufficiently timely to permit real-time implementation. Either their timely advice is received by subscribers too late, or their recommendations are made too late to permit real-time implementation. Ideally, you should either be able to maintain close touch with your advisory service on a daily basis or the recommendations provided in their newsletter should be so specific and with such close follow-up that telephone contact would be unnecessary.

3. **Objectives, Stops, Alternatives**
   A good advisory service should provide you with all three of these. Ideally you should have price or time objectives, stops and specific follow-up procedures that will leave you with alternatives regardless of market conditions. If you are going to pay an advisor, then make sure you are paying for a complete package. Some services are wonderful at getting you into the market, but vague and nonspecific when it comes to getting you out.

4. **Cost**

   The cost of some services may be prohibitive in terms of what you get. While it is true that each service is unique in the information it provides, the cost of what you get may not turn out to be effective in terms of how you use the information, or of the extent to which the information proves profitable. Unfortunately, it is impossible to know this in advance. Rather, you will need to make this evaluation at regular intervals once you have found a service that suits your needs.

5. **Portfolio Size**

   Some advisory services with excellent performance records have achieved their hypothetical results in a fashion that cannot be duplicated by most speculators. In some cases, they have taken on extremely large positions, scaled into the market holding losing positions, hypothetically purchased or sold extremely large numbers of contracts or added more and more margin to their hypothetical account until they have weathered most storms. Since this is not a realistic way for the average trader to approach the market, it is not suggested that you follow the work of a service such as this. I'm aware of several services (at least) that have practiced such procedures in one form or another (sometimes in all forms). Without naming names, I recommend you be aware.

   Realistically, most futures portfolios should not contain more than 5 to 10 positions at any point in time. That's just my orientation, but I think you'll find this approach makes sense for most speculators.

6. **Hotline**

   Does the service have a hotline that you can call at least daily in order to obtain the latest recommendations, updates and follow-ups? The recorder is a good way to keep in touch with your service and its recommendations. However, a hotline is not necessary if the service can maintain thorough follow-up in its newsletter. Note that some recorder hotlines are essentially useless, since they do not provide specific recommendations. Rather, they provide nothing but general comments.

7. Performance Record

You will observe that performance record is not one of the major items on my list, yet it is important. Provided the performance record is honestly reported and truly representative of the service's record, you should consider its history carefully. The would-be subscriber who looks merely at the bottom line may be in for a rude awakening when he or she actually subscribes to the service.

You must examine in close detail such items as the largest single loss, the largest single profit, the average loss, the average profit and the win/lose percentage ratio. The reasons for doing so should be abundantly clear to you if you have been reading previous chapters in this book carefully. It is important to remember that a service that makes most of its profits on a few highly profitable trades may not be the best service for you. The rule of thumb in assessing the potential of any service in your program is whether you can duplicate its results. If you can, then the service is for you. If, however, the results would be difficult for you to replicate, then you are best advised to look elsewhere.

8. Deduction for Commissions

Read the fine print! Some services do not deduct exceptionally large commissions from their performance records. Other services do not deduct any commissions from their performance records. There is no need for me to expand on this item. It is self-explanatory. The service you will want to follow *must* have a track record that closely resembles a realistic trading situation.

9. **Price Fills**

   Another significant item regarding realistic representation
   of recommendations is the area of hypothetical price fills.
   Some services claim recommendations being filled on entry
   and/or exit when, in fact, such fills may not have been
   possible at the stated price. Consider this in evaluating your
   subscription to a service.

10. **Which Markets Are Traded?**

    Some services specialize in only certain markets. It may
    be that the markets that are the specialty of a certain
    service are either too risky or too volatile for you. You
    can determine this fact from examining the performance
    record and from studying the service's promotional liter-
    ature. Also bear in mind that the service may make recom-
    mendations in particularly thin markets, which may also
    not be to your liking. Advisory service recommendations
    to a large audience in a thin market can certainly result
    in exceptionally bad price executions on entry and exit.
    Do not subscribe to a service that is not consistent with
    your needs, general expectations and orientation regarding
    specific markets covered.

TRUST YOURSELF

Too many traders, novice and experienced, have difficulty
trusting their own judgment and decisions. This is the insecurity
that breeds errors of the trader, as opposed to errors of the system.
Whether you subscribe to a good service, whether you have a good
system, whether you have a good broker, no help will come to
you if you cannot trust your decisions. Perhaps you have made
your decisions with the input of others, or perhaps you have made
them in isolation (probably the best way). If you cannot follow
through with confidence on your decisions, the end result will not
be to your liking.

It is not possible to teach self-assuredness or self-confidence. They can only be developed as a function of long and hard experience. However, to the trader who can develop the self-trust to forge ahead in spite of the chance that losses might be waiting just ahead will belong the ultimate victory.

SUMMARY

The different types of services were discussed drawing some meaningful and often misunderstood distinctions. The reader was advised to consider whether a service is necessary. The importance of self-trust and self-confidence were stressed.

Chapter
12

Brokers: Finding Them,
Keeping Them and
Working with Them

From my observation, one of the most misunderstood things about futures trading, aside from the placement orders, is the relationship between broker and client. In the old days, it was believed that in order to profit from stock or futures trading it was necessary to have a good broker. Today, there are still brokerage firms whose main thrust of advertising is their brokers' expertise in selecting profitable trades with the assistance of the brokerage houses' research departments.

Unfortunately, such brokers are indeed a rare commodity and, generally speaking, I suspect that most brokers' advice is not significantly better than that of their clients. This not to say that brokerage houses are lacking in good commodity research. It is, however, quite evident to me that regardless of how good a broker's research or opinions may be, once these opinions get into the hands of their customers, once the interaction between broker and client begins to take hold, there are many scenarios that can seriously undermine the effectiveness of the trading approach.

Commodity traders through the years have gone through a series of love/hate relationships with brokers. Back in the 1960s brokers supposedly had the inside line to many of the fundamental developments in the futures market. At that time, customers were very selective about the firm with which they did business. Certain firms were felt to be particularly adept in the metals or tropical commodities.

Today, many of these distinctions have fallen by the wayside. In fact, many individuals who in the 1960s thought that brokers should be advisors, have now reversed direction and feel that brokers should give no advice. In part, some of these changes are due to *the de facto deregulation of brokerage commissions* and the ensuing discount commission war. Other issues that have shaped the current status of the commodity brokerage business include *the decrease in futures trading volume in the traditional markets,* and *the corresponding spiral of volume increase in the financial and currencies markets.*

In order to fully understand the relationship between broker and client, it is important to understand the differences between types of customers. These factors can interact to produce a positive, negative or neutral result. The relationship between broker and client can prove to be your greatest asset or greatest liability. This is why I strongly suggest that you do not take the issue of selecting a broker too lightly. Many decisions must be made, and they must be made correctly as early in the game as possible.

WHO ARE YOU AND WHERE ARE YOU GOING?

The first decision you must make is a decision about the kind of trader you are and would like to be, and where you plan to go with your trading. There are essentially several types of traders. A discussion of their characteristics follows.

1. **The Novice**
   The trader with little or no experience who feels nervous, uncertain and insecure and is likely lacking in knowledge. Such an individual can either be thrown into the waters or he can be nurtured, educated and assisted by association

with the right type of broker. Such an individual would be best dealing with a broker who is patient, not too terribly busy and familiar with the details that concern the novice trader. Specifically, such information as appropriate placement of orders, margin requirements, understanding purchase and sale statements, contract specifications, reports and an elementary knowledge of various trading systems would be helpful to such an individual.

2. **Experienced Short-Term Trader**
   The experienced short-term trader is usually an individual who has considerable experience, who is primarily interested in quick trading (usually intraday or over a period of several days) and who has sufficient knowledge. Some of these individuals may require price quotes, others may require no quotes whatsoever, and need only have a broker who can execute orders promptly, efficiently, and at reasonably good prices. Such an individual would require, and would, in fact, often demand, no input whatsoever from his or her broker. Not only would there be no time for input, but generally speaking such an individual is very certain of his or her trades and would not want to be swayed by accepting other input.

3. **The Long-Term Trader**
   Such an individual would not trade very often and might require some specialized services from a broker such as statistical information and fundamental data ordinarily available from brokerage houses. Such an individual would do well to go with a brokerage firm that has a strong fundamental orientation as well as the ability to obtain and provide the necessary statistics promptly.

4. **The Independent Trader**
   Regardless of market orientation, long-term, short-term, fundamental or technical, many traders prefer to be totally

independent and seek no input whatsoever from their broker. Such independent individuals are best off selecting a broker who provides minimal input and whose primary function is that of an order taker.

Essentially, these are the four types of traders common in today's market. As you can see, most traders generally align themselves in two major classes, those who seek to have brokerage input and those who are not interested in any information they can obtain from their broker. Naturally, the broker who provides information, quotes, opinions, etc., should be reimbursed for additional services, whereas the broker who provides nothing but price fills should be able to provide lower commissions. Hence, the distinction between "full-service brokers" and "discount brokers."

DISCOUNT VERSUS FULL SERVICE

It is often necessary for traders to make their own choices as to the type of broker with whom they wish to have an account. Essentially, the choice is between the so-called full-service broker and the discounter. There are some distinct differences between the two types, although with the passage of time many of the distinctions are becoming less noticeable in terms of service. Specifically here are a few words about each type of brokerage concern.

Full-Service Broker

The full-service broker is the traditional type of brokerage firm that provides, as the name applies, full service. By full service, they mean virtually anything from stocks, bonds, futures, money market funds, tax shelters, options, research publications, advice, etc. The full-service stock and commodity firm provides these services in both areas, whereas the full-service futures brokerage firm provides these services only in the area of futures trading. Full-service futures brokerage firms pride themselves on producing considerable research, providing price quotes to clients through their brokers, and frequently maintaining one or several managed account programs for their customers.

Discount Brokerage Firms

Discount brokers, both in stocks and commodities, charge significantly lower commission rates than do full-service firms, since they generally do not provide costly research and research publications that full-service firms produce. Recently, some discounters have moved to a sliding discount scale under which they provide some additional customer services such as research and broker input, but at a lower rate than full-service firms. Similarly, many full-service firms are now discounting their commissions to customers who do not require the use of research, price quotation, and/or considerable broker input.

In recent years, the brokerage industry both in stocks and futures has become highly competitive. The commission price war has gone just about as far as it can go, given the present cost of commissions to the floor broker and back-office expenses. For most futures traders, the key considerations in opening an account with a given firm are threefold. Here are several points to consider carefully when you select a broker. Consider these in addition to your need for broker input or for independent trading.

1. **Safety of Capital**
   In selecting a brokerage firm, be sure that your capital will be safe. Before you send money, get some references and make certain you are dealing with a firm that has backing. Low commissions are important, but financial stability is more important.

2. **Commissions**
   I could write an entire chapter on the subject of commissions. I am sure, however, that the topic can be covered sufficiently in a matter of paragraphs.

The simple fact of the matter is that you will need to decide on what commissions you want to pay depending on the services you require. Certainly if you are an individual who calls for a price quote many times a day, or if you require input from your broker (information, statistics, etc.), then you should expect to pay more, since this is only fair for the brokerage firm. However, if you are a trader who makes his or her own decisions, requiring nothing from your broker other than prompt, efficient and fair price fills, then the discount broker is what you need.

Take the time to evaluate the services offered by the various firms you are considering and make your judgments based upon your needs. You can expect to pay lower commissions if the number of trades per month is relatively low. Don't be afraid to shop around, and by all means feel free to visit and/or interview the firms you are considering. I think you can learn a great deal by actually visiting the office of the firm with whom you are considering opening an account.

3. **Various Special Needs**

I have indicated earlier that different traders have different needs. If, for example, I were looking for a brokerage firm that could be helpful to me with my short-term or daytrading, I would look for a firm that could fill and report back my orders as quickly as possible. There are distinct differences among brokerage firms when compared along these lines. Ideally for such a trader, the faster the order comes back, the better.

On the other hand, I may be interested in the fundamentals and timely information regarding changes in them, and/or commercial activity in the various markets. Some firms have very close ties to commercials and/or monitor fundamentals and commercial activity very closely. You can find out who can meet this special need by asking questions not only of the firms themselves, but other experienced traders, as well.

Finally, you may be interested in trading only one particular market, such as Treasury bond futures, or Standard and Poor's futures. You may find it better to deal with a brokerage firm that specializes in a particular market you may wish to follow. The advantages here would be prompt price fills, quick reporting back with your fill, good information on the fundamentals or pit conditions for the given market (if you want it) and, oftentimes, lower commissions.

DISCRETIONARY ACCOUNTS WITH BROKERS

An area that I have not mentioned until now is the discretionary or managed-account program. Such programs essentially take all of the decision-making functions and controls away from the speculator, and put them into the hands of a program, group or individual who, by virtue of various factors, will exercise control over the account. With the exception of making such decisions as adding money to the account, taking money out of the account, or closing the account, the individual has no input.

For many traders or would-be traders this can ultimately prove to be the best approach since it leaves little room for error on the part of the speculator. On the other hand, the individual places his or her trust and faith in the hands of another trader, for better or for worse. For the individual who seeks to trade futures indirectly, who has neither the time, discipline, patience or skill, such programs might be best.

SUMMING IT ALL UP

You can see from the foregoing discussion that the job of finding a broker and a brokerage house is not only considerably more involved than most people believe it to be, but it is also a very important task, the result of which can ultimately be to your benefit or to your detriment. For many years, speculators and investors have misperceived both the importance of having the right brokerage house and the importance of having the right broker. Furthermore, you can see that there is no single right answer to both of these issues. The right broker and the right brokerage house are a matter of individual preference which should ideally be based upon individual need, experience, trading style and broker/client interaction.

Before closing this chapter, I would like to give you just a few thoughts about broker/client interaction. Brokers and customers come in many different forms and personalities. Some customers are very demanding, inconsiderate and impatient. Other customers are passive, easily intimidated and generally shy. Some brokers are patient and empathetic, others are intimidating, pushy and impatient.

The many different types of customers and brokers and their different interactions allow for many different types of broker/client relationships. For the relatively new, inexperienced or veteran trader lacking self-confidence and discipline, the relationship between client and broker can be a key element in the formula for success. It can also be another stop on the road to failure.

I have made a number of claims about the importance of the broker/client relationship. Now let's get specific about the relationship and look at some precise details about the interaction and its potential consequences, both positive and negative.

HOW CAN BROKERS INFLUENCE CLIENTS

The ultimate fact of the matter is the more you trade the more your broker makes. It's an undeniable fact of life.

When you are looking to buy a computer, an automobile, or any other piece of merchandise, the salesperson is often very emphatic in telling you that their product is the one you want to buy "because it has. . . ." In other words, it is the job of the salesperson to sell you on a particular item. Whether or not the item is ultimately precisely what you need can only be determined by you, both in advance and, unfortunately, after the fact.

You can only hope that with a little bit of knowledge and research you will make the right decision. Your decision must be based upon many variables and, frequently, an influential salesperson can sway you in a given direction. Ultimately, the direction in which you are swayed may not be the best direction for you to take.

Many commodity brokers are salespersons. They research trades from many available sources and decide upon a particular course of action based upon their analyses and their interpretations or the analyses and interpretations of their brokerage firms. They then suggest various trades to their customers. In order to effectively sell the customer on a given trade or trades they need to have at their disposal the facts and figures, both technical and fundamental, that the customer will naturally want in order to be convinced that the trade is indeed for them. Selling clients on a trade was a very common practice in the 1960s and 1970s. In spite of its relative dormancy, it appears to be resurfacing again in recent years.

I have received considerable mail advertising from firms seeking to acquire business on the basis of "special situations" in certain futures markets and/or various low-risk strategies in some of the markets. In most cases, their research is well-documented, both technically and fundamentally. In some cases, however, these individuals are ruthless operators who will present a very positive picture about a certain market, overstating the potential rewards and understating the potential risks. Certainly the buyer must beware and fend for him- or herself.

This type of advertising appeals to the baser instincts of the public. Many people are attracted to such selling programs, many of which are destined to failure. While I am not suggesting you ignore all attempts by brokers to secure your business, I do believe that you must be careful about the firms with whom you plan to deal. You've probably heard about people losing their life savings on futures trading programs they've been attracted to by mail advertisements. Any scheme that sounds too good to be true, too difficult to understand, or like too much of a sure thing, is likely to be one you should avoid. A few simple steps, a few simple questions, a check of credentials and references could avoid much agony and loss.

Yes, brokers can and do influence their clients, but, for the most part, such influence is not with malice. The good broker is interested in helping his or her client profit, since this will serve both parties well. However, even good brokers do not know many of the answers. Ultimately, *the answer is up to you and you alone.*

SUMMARY

This chapter reviewed in depth the importance of selecting an appropriate broker. In addition, the value of working with a broker was seen in terms of potential profits or losses. The issue of taking advice from a broker as opposed to being an independent trader was given detailed discussion. Finally, a comparison was drawn between so-called full-service brokers and discount brokers in order to assist the reader in selecting the brokerage firm that will best assist his or her trading.

The issue of selecting a broker and a brokerage firm has for too long been given only passing consideration by traders and investors. I maintain that this is one of the single most important choices a speculator can make. Therefore, I strongly suggest taking time to review your possible choices, as well as taking care in making a final selection. The value of a beneficial relationship with a broker and brokerage firm is so significant that I urge you to keep an open mind, even after your decisions have been made. Don't be afraid to change to a different broker or firm if you have the slightest inclination that your path to success is not being facilitated by the choices you have made.

It is unfortunate that the "bottom line" for many investors is strictly the dollar amount of commissions they must pay. Nothing could be more absurd than a decision based entirely upon cost. While it is true that the cost of commissions is a major factor in the overall dollar return from your trading, cost is not nearly as important as prompt and fair price executions, professionalism, accurate information when you need it and lack of interference with your decisions (unless you request opinions or feedback on your decisions). It is wrong to sacrifice everything in the name of cheap commissions. What may seem cheap in the short run could prove costly in the long run!

Chapter

13

What You Need to Know about Placing Orders

One of the most critically important, but least understood aspects of futures trading is the use of price orders. Oftentimes traders misunderstand the meaning of certain orders and, upon receiving a bad order fill, tend to blame their broker. In fact, a thorough knowledge of order placement can circumvent much aggravation, as well as many poor price fills.

In order better to understand orders, let's first trace an order from its inception to its culmination. Let's assume you call your broker, placing an order to buy one contract of March Treasury bond futures "at the market." Specifically this means you will buy at whatever price can be obtained for you when your order reaches the floor of the exchange or the trading pit (the difference to be explained later on).

The order-entry process begins with your call to your broker. You pick up the phone and call your broker. "Buy one March T Bond at the market," is the instruction. Depending upon the type of trading you do and the type of broker you have, you will either hang up the phone or you will hold on for your price fill.

When your broker receives the order, he or she will write an order ticket containing your account number and your specific order. The ticket will then be time-stamped. Your broker will call the order down to the floor of the exchange, where the ticket will be similarly written and handed to a runner.

The runner will take the ticket to the pit broker who will then execute your order, write the price fill on the ticket, and hand it back to the runner. The runner will take it back to the order desk on the floor. The floor desk will report back to your broker, and your broker will then give you your price fill, either while you are waiting on the telephone or by calling you.

If you are doing business with a broker who can fill your order using arbitrage methods, the procedure just described will be somewhat different. Once your broker has the order and calls it down to the floor an individual at the order desk on the floor will hand-signal the pit trader to execute your order. The pit trader will then execute it and, by hand signal, report the fill back to the order desk. In this way you can very frequently have your order filled and reported back to you most often in less than one minute. Arbitrage techniques are becoming more common in very active markets such as Standard & Poor's futures and Treasury bond futures.

Other types of orders such as those above the market, below the market or conditional orders are executed in essentially the same way. Since they are resting orders, however, they are not filled immediately. Rather, they are brought in to the pit and given to the pit broker who keeps them in his "deck." The deck consists of small cards on which the pit broker keeps track of orders he or she has filled and the orders he or she needs to fill. Now let's take a look at the different types of orders that are possible and some of the intricacies that may be involved with some of these orders.

MARKET ORDER

A market order does exactly what it says. Placing an order to buy or sell at the market means that your order will be executed at the best possible price as soon as the pit broker has received it. In an active market, such orders are safe to use and very common.

However, you must understand that in a less active market, such an order should only be used when it is absolutely vital that you have the order filled immediately.

If, for example, you place an order to buy at the market, but there are no price offers close to the last trade, the floor trader or pit broker will continue to bid higher and higher until your market order has been filled. In a thin or inactive market this could be at virtually any price. Therefore, your order will frequently not get filled at a very good price compared to what you think you should have gotten. Be very careful when using market orders in thin markets. In fact, it is best not to use market orders in such cases.

MARKET ON CLOSE (MOC) ORDERS

A market on close order is an instruction to the pit broker to execute an order for you, to buy or to sell, during the last one minute of trading. Your order is frequently executed during the last few seconds of trading and, in most cases, is not too much different than the closing price. Very frequently such orders are filled in the closing price range. On occasion, MOC orders do not result in particularly good fills. It has been my experience that MOC orders in most active markets do not result in terribly bad price fills. Several ticks difference between what you expected and what you received can occur.

On occasion, an MOC order will work to your advantage. This is particularly true when a market is near limit up or limit down. Assume, for an example, that you would like to buy at the end of the day. Assume that the market is weak. In such a case, the market will often drop even lower on the close as those who were buying during the day have MOC orders to sell. If you are short and have a MOC order to buy or if you want to go net long, chances are you will get a reasonably good fill, often at or close to limit down.

The reverse often holds true with MOC orders to sell. In other words, if the market is sharply higher and you have a long position you would like to liquidate by the close or a short you would like to establish, this could be an ideal situation. Frequently in a market that has been strong all day, there will be a rush to the upside bringing prices close to or possibly limit up. This happens because those who were short for the day rush in to cover their short positions. There will be buying, which will run the price up. Since you will be selling, you may get a better price fill than you expected. MOC orders should also be avoided in thin markets.

MARKET "NOT HELD"

This is an instruction to the floor broker to fill your order as best he or she can and that you will not hold the pit broker accountable in the event of a poor fill. Such orders are generally not used by the public or for small amounts of contracts. Don't trouble the pit broker with such an order unless you have a large number of contracts to buy or sell.

MARKET ON THE OPEN ORDER

This is a very simple, self-explanatory order. Essentially, it is an order entered before the opening to buy at the market as soon as the market opens. Typically, there is a great deal of activity on market opens but in thin markets this could result in a reasonably bad price fill. Some market analysts and advisors have strong sentiment against buying on the open. They feel that the opening is not necessarily a good reflection of market activity. Indeed, on many occasions in the past, traders have witnessed significant reversals after a strong opening in a given direction.

Certainly, if our market entry was on the buy side on a sharply higher opening during one of the reversal type days, then we would indeed be in jeopardy, or vice versa during a sharply lower opening. However as I will demonstrate to you in a later chapter, the opening price in all markets is very important and I have developed a specific technique for using opening prices as a means of predicting significant levels of support and resistance.

STOP ORDERS

There are a number of stop orders. Stop orders are those which are generally either above or below the market. They are:

Buy Stop

This is an order to buy at a given price above the market. When the indicated price is hit, your order becomes a market order and it is filled at the best price possible thereafter. Such orders are used to exit a short position or to enter a long position on market strength.

Sell Stop

This is an order to sell at a price below the market. Once the price is hit, your order is filled at that price or at the best price possible. Such orders are used to exit a long position or to enter a short position on market weakness.

Stop Loss

The term "stop loss" is applied to a position that offsets an existing position. Such an order is designed to limit a loss, hence the name "stop loss." Orders are not entered as stop loss orders, but rather in the variety of ways described below. Hence, the term "stop loss" is a generic term that could be applied to orders above or below the market.

Stop Limit

The stop limit order is a specific type of stop order used either above or below the market. A sell stop limit means that you want to sell below the market, but at *no lower than the price of your limit.* In other words, you must be filled at your price or not at all. This is a good way to guarantee a fill at a certain price, but if the market goes through your price and does not trade at it, or the order cannot be filled even at the limit price, you will not be filled. You may not get the protection you want if you are using this as a stop loss. The reverse holds true for stop limit orders above the market.

Stop limits should be used when you want to avoid a bad fill, or when you are working with a precise technical level. I do not recommend using stop limits for the purpose of stop losses.

Stop Close Only

This is an instruction to sell or buy within the closing minute of trading. A sell stop close only order will be executed at or below the given price during the closing minute. A buy stop close only will be executed at or above the given price during the last minute of trading. Many times the fill price will not be in agreement with the last tick or settlement price due to the time span during which a stop close only order can be filled.

Fill or Kill Order

This order is not used very frequently. It has its merits, however, a fill or kill order is essentially an instruction to the pit broker to fill your order at a given price within a matter of minutes or to cancel your order. It is a way of placing a price order close to the market in an effort to obtain close to an immediate feedback on disposition of your order.

Such an order is best used when you wish to enter or exit a position quickly, but rather than doing so at the market you want to do so at a given price in order to avoid the possibility of a poor price fill. Fill or kill orders can be used in thin markets, or in markets that have been hovering around a certain price level, but for some reason will not come to the price level at which you are seeking to enter or exit a position.

Good Till Cancelled Orders

A good till canceled order means just that. An order is in the market until you cancel it. As a matter of procedure, most brokerage firms clear the books of orders at the end of every day's trading unless these orders are specified as good till canceled orders.

Most short-term traders do not find it necessary to use good till canceled orders. They can be used when you will be out of touch with the market, but I strongly suggest against trading when you are not in touch with the markets. Therefore, you will not need to use a good till canceled order. Such orders are much more common in the stock market.

SUMMARY

Price orders are very important inasmuch as they will affect the price at which you buy or sell. Naturally, this will also affect your bottom line. One thing to remember with regard to order placement is that you must be specific and decisive. Don't get a bad reputation with your broker by being unclear, saying one thing, but meaning another.

Finally, remember that *in many cases, existing orders must be found in the pit brokers deck before you can replace them with another order!* This could markedly affect your price fill. Therefore, if you have an existing order that must be canceled and replaced with a market order, remember that your existing order will need to be found and removed so that there is no duplication. This takes time. The result could be a poor price fill. Therefore, if you suspect that you will need to cancel a replace, cancel as soon as you can then enter your market order when ready. This will make certain your order is filled immediately and your resulting price fill could be better. Remember the cancel procedure. It could save you much grief and much money as well.

Chapter
14

What You Need to Know about Computers

With the tremendous growth and popularity of home computer systems in recent years, it is almost a heresy to say that very few individuals actually need computers. While it is true that personal computer systems have made many things easier for the businessperson, I suspect that their use, with a few specific exceptions, has been generally overrated.

Today, for example, there are many novice traders who feel that they cannot be successful in futures trading without a computer quote system and/or a computer trading system. I'm from the "old school." I emphatically insist that success is not computer-dependent in today's futures markets. It is perfectly possible for virtually any aspiring futures trader to be successful without a computer, without a "quote system" and without a computerized trading system.

The public relations and advertising jobs unleashed upon the public worldwide have apparently had their desired effect in attracting many new followers to the fold. My long-standing point of view is that the decision to buy a computer for futures trading should receive considerable deliberation before a commitment is made. Not only are computers expensive, but their maintenance is not gratis. The overall expense of purchasing, maintaining and operating a computer may be prohibitive to the new futures trader.

These days, it seems more and more that the decision is not whether one should get a computer trading system, but rather which system will do the job the best. Although my advice to a good majority of futures traders is that they don't really need a computer system or a computerized trading method, I know that my words will fall on deaf ears. If you have already set your mind on buying a computer, then, at the very least, follow some guidelines in making your decision. Since it will possibly be difficult, if not impossible, for me to change anyone's mind about their perceived need of a computer, then at least, consider some guidelines based on personal experience in this area.

I will cover the subject in as simple terms as possible, since I know that computer jargon can be quite difficult to follow. It should also be remembered with the rapid changes occurring almost daily in the field of computer technology, any specific comments I could make about a particular system or systems would certainly be out of date by the time you have purchased and read this book. Therefore, my comments will be generic, and hopefully in this way they will have a longer shelf life.

MAKING THE DECISION

Assuming you have not already made your decision about purchasing a computer system, I suggest you take a number of points into consideration before you reach your decision. If you have already made your decision, but have not purchased a system, consider these points, as well, since they may affect your final selections.

1. **What Will the System Do for You?**
   If your futures trading system is highly complex and requires considerable mathematical manipulation on a frequent basis, then you have no choice but to purchase

a computer. In addition, if research of futures systems and methods is what you intend to do, then the computer will be absolutely necessary. In each case, remember that an additional and significant cost of the system will be the data and the programming.

You may do the programming yourself or you may purchase some prepackaged software. The cost of data is still something to consider when determining your total expense. You must also remember that continuous data updates will be required if you plan to use the system in real time and/or if you plan to update your research regularly.

Unless these two significant computer applications are your goals, the odds are that what you wish to accomplish can probably be done with a sophisticated hand-held calculator, or with a very small microcomputer at significantly lower cost than a full-fledged personal computer system.

In order to fully determine your need for a computer, you should also attempt to evaluate your future needs based on the requirements of the system or systems you plan to use. A good rule of thumb is to determine how long it takes you to generate your trading signals each day. Many systems can be updated manually in a matter of minutes every day, whereas others may require several hours to produce trading signals. Certainly, several hours of calculations every day can be quite tedious and a computer would clearly prove cost-effective in such a case.

Since I recommend that novices use only simple trading systems requiring minimal time input and expense, a conservative approach to an otherwise high-risk venture is usually a sensible balance. Assuming that you have decided to purchase a computer system after considering the expense, usefulness, maintenance costs, programming cost, and data costs, you may now read on to some of the other general areas of importance. If you have decided not to purchase a computer system, you can skip the balance of this chapter.

2. **What Will You Need in a System?**
   The weak link in any computer system is not necessarily the computer memory, but rather storage and printer capabilities. This is so because the printer is normally the slowest peripheral device and the storage device(s) the most used. If you are like most futures traders, you will want to purchase a system that will provide good graphics in hard-copy form (i.e., on the printer) so that you may study charts, chart patterns and price relationships. You will also want to study large amounts of data.

   Even if chart patterns are not what you wish to analyze, you will need your printer for getting hard-copy results of any research programs you plan to run on your data. Therefore, I would consider the printer one of the most important links in the chain and certainly the most vulnerable one.

   When buying a system, attempt to get a printer of reasonably high speed and very high resolution. The storage device(s) is (are) also important. Storage is discussed below.

3. **Storage.**
   One of the most important features of any computer system you intend to buy is the amount of data it will store on disk. With more and more historical data added to the base with each passing day, as well as with the growing trend for intraday data analysis, the more storage you can get, the better off you will be in terms of saved labor. There are many different types of storage systems available. These range from tape storage to floppy disk to hard disk.

   Ideally, hard disk storage of approximately 30 megabytes should be sufficient to keep on file data for virtually every futures contract on a daily basis for the last 15 years. Having such storage capabilities will permit you to analyze virtually any program on every market in your database without having to change disks. This will permit you to be away from your computer system doing other productive work while the system is busy "crunching numbers." I would suggest that if additional money is going to be spent, it should be spent on storage as opposed to memory.

If computer programs are efficiently written in an assembler language or in some other noninterpretive computer instruction, then smaller memory will be sufficient with larger storage being more important. Large storage is an absolute necessity for those wishing to perform complex, historical analyses or intraday studies.

4. **CPU (Mainframe)**
The CPU (central processing unit) is the heart of the system hardware. Memory size is an important consideration when researching price patterns. Although many computer users get carried away with large computer memory, efficient programming can circumvent the need for large memory. With the cost of add-on memory becoming lower all the time, I would suggest that you consider the cost to memory ratio in making your final decision. If you can considerably more memory at reasonably low cost then, by all means, do so. But remember that storage is more important than memory.

5. **Compatibility**
Many good computer systems on today's market can be had at very low prices, but some are not essentially compatible with the software or data stream provided by the popular computer services. The trend has been for most data to be written specifically for use with the most popular software and the most popular computer systems. In view of these limitations, your choices of hardware will probably be very limited since the cost of producing new software to accommodate an off-brand computer system may be prohibitive.

Some individuals may wish to use a specific computerized trading system produced by a given software firm. In

such cases, the trader will be constrained by the limitations
of the hardware system for which the software was originally written.

The issue of compatibility is becoming more important
every day. While there have been many upstart software
firms and "clone" hardware systems, the battle has slowly
but surely been won by a few of the larger hardware firms
and only several of the manufacturers of "clone type"
systems have survived.

Today, much good research and trading systems software is written for only two or three specific hardware
systems. Though this is a fairly typical result of competition, it does, unfortunately, limit the choices of hardware
available to you.

INVENT THE WHEEL OR RE-INVENT THE WHEEL?

The almost continuous stream of futures trading software that
now dominates the marketplace has turned from a slow trickle
into a virtual waterfall of programs. Competition is becoming
greater every day and rarely a day passes without a new program
or system being presented to the public for sale or lease. The
response of the public has been quite positive and futures software sales have been booming.

In some cases, there may be so many users of a particular
system that this could, to a certain extent, affect its operations.
However, the large number of alternatives and competitive systems
on today's market makes the likelihood of too many traders
following any one particular system rather small. This speaks
favorably about the possibility of profiting from one of the
commercially available systems.

The independent trader will probably want to avoid most
commercially available trading systems in favor of developing his
or her own trading approach using concepts and techniques he
or she has developed. This is, of course, the ideal application of

computer systems and the results may justify the entire cost of the system many times over.

You should also know that if you are interested in trading software development, there are some utility programs available that may cut down considerably on your work. Specifically, you can purchase a prewritten program that will allow you to input various parameters for test purposes. You may then generate hypothetical trading results more quickly and specifically without having to go through all of the programming work from start to finish. With the passage of time, I am certain that many more programs will be available that, ultimately may virtually eliminate most of the individual research required in software development.

Although the decision to develop or use prewritten software is certainly an individual one, the rapid changes and accelerating progress in futures trading software research make it worth your while to consider a prewritten program as opposed to developing your own systems. Unfortunately, the purchase of a prewritten program eliminates much of the challenge of this game. Yet, the challenge of making profits is still the greatest one, indeed! Consider also the possibility of modifying existing software to more closely suit your needs or, perhaps, to vastly improve its performance.

COMPUTERIZED QUOTE SYSTEMS

The days of the large mechanical quote board that clicked and ticked away in the broker's office are almost history. The familiar sound of rapidly changing prices has been replaced by the complete silence of the green screen and the occasional beeping of a computer reminding its master that something of importance has occurred. The hand drawn chart has been replaced by the familiar dot matrix of the computer printer, and the "good, old fashioned" colored lines and colored pencils are now also victims of progress.

Yet, in spite of our wonderful technology, there are still many,

many significant differences between quote systems. Virtually no barrier has been a significant one if cost is no object. The single best way to determine the type of quotation system best suited for your purposes is to "test drive" them. If you cannot arrange for a no-cost trial period, then attempt to visit a broker or friend who has a system and use it for a while to see how you relate to it. Different systems have different strengths and weaknesses. Certainly you would hate to purchase a system and be stuck with it if it is not ideally suited to the precise applications you require.

SUMMARY

The advent of home computer systems has broadened the scope of futures traders. We can now analyze massive amounts of data in a matter of minutes. The net effect, however, has now been minimized since the advantage is now available to virtually all traders whether with their own computer systems or via the purchase of research performed by various services.

The computer trading revolution may, however, be illusory. Many traders, particularly novices, are convinced that they cannot attain success in futures without a computer. This chapter debunked the computer dependency myth. It provided some specific guidelines upon which to evaluate computer systems. I emphasized the point that a computer *is not necessary for success.* I outlined some reasons for buying or not buying a computer system.

Part 4

Advanced Trading Strategies and Techniques

Chapter
15

Advanced Concepts
in Moving Averages

My earlier discussion of moving averages illustrated the very basic applications and timing indicators of this technique. In recent years, the availability of high-powered computers at reasonably low prices has spawned many variations on the theme of moving averages. I have worked extensively with moving averages of highs and lows as opposed to moving averages of closing prices, finding this technique exceptionally good at isolating support and resistance levels, as well as possible turning points in the markets.

For those who wish to pursue more advanced applications of the moving average techniques, I offer this chapter, which contains two moving average techniques. They both appear to have good potential as trading systems, but they are not offered here as such, since specific money-management rules and stop-loss procedures would need to be added to the basic timing signals. Those who wish to develop these as trading systems, should do more research on stop and risk procedures.

THE MOVING AVERAGE CHANNEL (MAC)

The Moving Average Channel (MAC) is a concept that was developed by Richard Donchian in the 1950s. Instead of plotting just the moving average of closing prices, or for that matter of several closing prices, Donchian suggested plotting the moving averages of high and low prices of each time unit. The result was a price channel or band containing two moving averages, one of highs and one of lows.

I have found the technique to be especially interesting and I have researched its possible applications. I found, for example, that the channel can work very well for the purpose of finding support and resistance. The MAC acts as support when prices decline in a bull market and as resistance when prices rally in a bear market. Figures 15–1, 15–2, and 15–3 show the channel, the channel with price, and various rallies to resistance and declines to support in established bull and bear markets.

The application of this technique is rather straightforward in terms of finding support and resistance. However, my work strongly suggests that more specific applications could be developed in terms of timing. Note the following characteristics of the moving average channel:

1. The moving average channel of 10 units of the high and 8 units of the low appears to be the most practical. Others are either too short or too long.
2. When a market has started a bullish move, corrections within that move tend to find support at either extreme of the channel or within the channel (i.e. price above channel).
3. In a bearish move, rallies tend to find resistance at either extreme of the channel or within the channel itself (i.e. price below channel).
4. Once price bars begin to appear fully outside of the channel on the upside, it is probable that a bullish move has started.
5. Once price bars begin to appear fully outside the bottom of the channel, it is probable that a downside move has started.

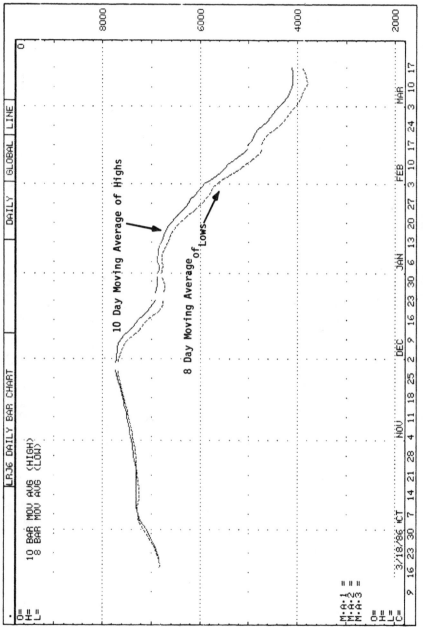

FIGURE 15–1 MOVING AVERAGE CHANNEL

(Reprinted with Permission of Commodity Quote Graphics)

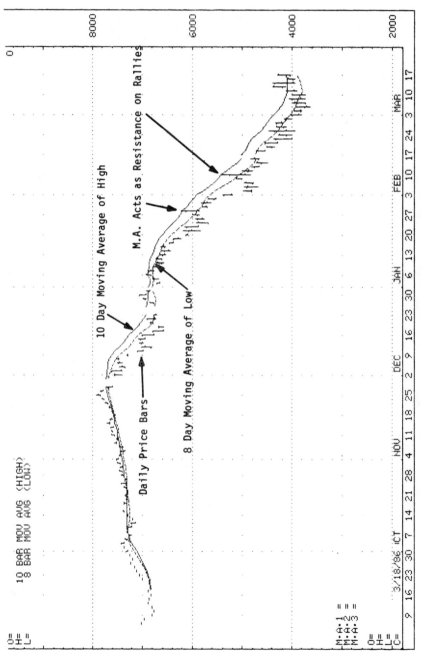

FIGURE 15–2 MOVING AVERAGE CHANNEL WITH PRICE
(Reprinted with Permission of Commodity Quote Graphics)

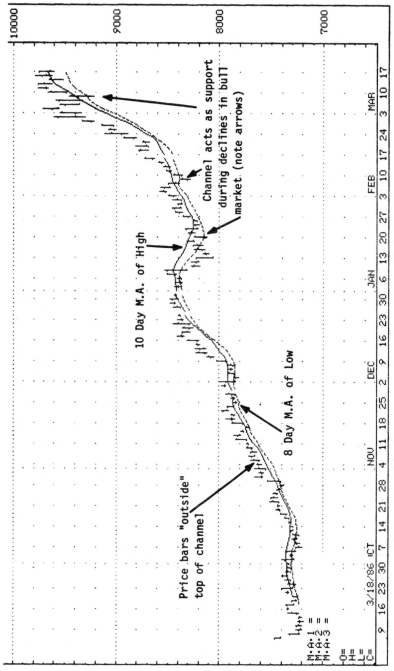

FIGURE 15-3 MOVING AVERAGE CHANNEL WITH VARIOUS RALLIES
(Reprinted with Permission of Commodity Quote Graphics)

These are the basic applications that I discovered. In and of themselves, I believe they have good potential value for the speculator. They help the speculator to form an opinion as to whether prices have changed trend, or if they remain in a previously established trend.

One More Step

If we take one more step with the moving average channel technique, adding to it a three-period moving average of closing prices, we arrive at a technique that appears to have great potential as a trading system. Essentially, the addition of the three period moving average of closing prices allows you to determine, numerically, when prices have seemingly lost their momentum within the existing channel and are likely to change direction. This is a way of determining, if you will, when the market has "run out of gas" on the upside or downside.

Figure 15–4 illustrates this technique, showing the potential buy and sell signals using the indicator and relating these to an actual price chart showing the hypothetical buy and sell points. Since the technique determines when prices have probably turned higher or lower, the speculator capable of assuming larger risk can use this system in a reversal sense, following every signal, being in the market at all times, and thereby employing this technique for money-management purposes. The drawback here would be that losses may sometimes get very large. Yet, profits would, at times, also be very large. Figures 15–5, 15–6 ,and 15–7 offer some further illustrations of this technique with the understanding that they are still being developed as a trading system.

MOVING AVERAGE TRADING BAND (MATB)

Another, and most interesting, application of the moving average is its use as a trading band. Recent applications of the

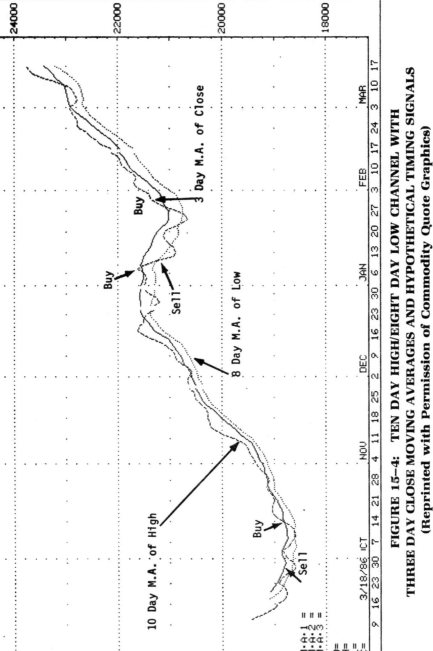

**FIGURE 15–4: TEN DAY HIGH/EIGHT DAY LOW CHANNEL WITH
THREE DAY CLOSE MOVING AVERAGES AND HYPOTHETICAL TIMING SIGNALS
(Reprinted with Permission of Commodity Quote Graphics)**

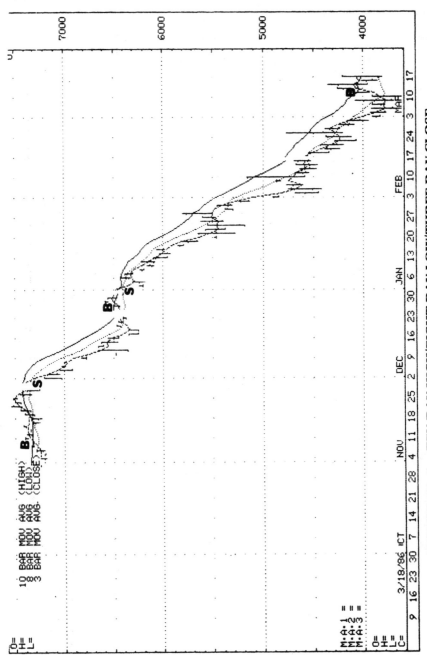

**FIGURE 15–5: TEN DAY HIGH/EIGHT DAY LOW/THREE DAY CLOSE
M. A. CHANNEL SIGNALS (B = BUY, S = SELL)
(Reprinted with Permission of Commodity Quote Graphics)**

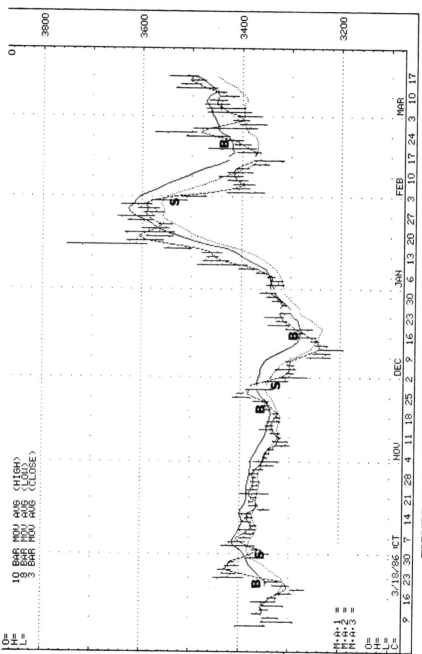

FIGURE 15–6: TEN DAY HIGH/EIGHT DAY LOW/THREE DAY CLOSE
M. A. CHANNEL SIGNALS (B = BUY, S = SELL)
(Reprinted with Permission of Commodity Quote Graphics)

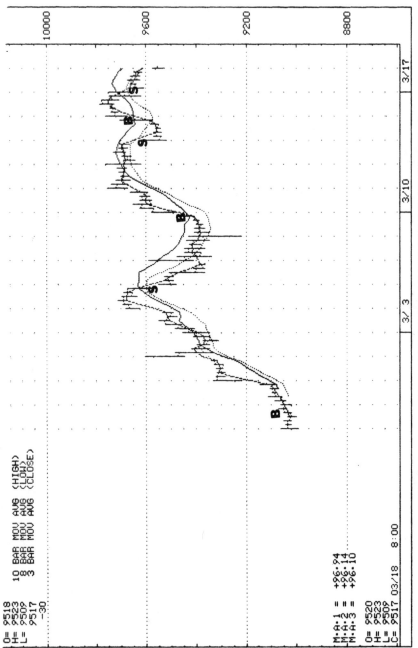

**FIGURE 15–7: TEN HIGH/EIGHT LOW//THREE CLOSE M. A.
CHANNEL AND TIMING SIGNALS (B = BUY, S = SELL)—HOURLY CHART
(Reprinted with Permission of Commodity Quote Graphics)**

trading-band concept incorporate closing prices and a percentage price band above and beyond the moving average. In other words, the closing price is used to determine a given moving average, and a percentage band above and below the closing price is constructed as a timing band within which prices tend to move back and forth as they form support and resistance usually at upper and lower ends of the channel.

Figures 15–8, and 15–9 illustrate two markets using a band of prices above and below the moving average. In this case, I have employed a moving average of five days and a channel of 1.5 percent above the closing price and 0.7 percent below the closing price. The concept illustrated here is fairly simple. Essentially, it suggests that the upper end of the channel tends to serve as resistance and the lower end of the channel or band tends to serve as support. I have indicated by arrows the examples of these levels.

For many years I have considered the opening price to be rather important. This runs contrary to the teachings and preachings of many traders, who feel that market openings should not be used for establishing positions. There is a subtle difference between my approach and theirs. While I am not disputing the possibility that bad price fills may be obtained by trading on the opening, I am saying that the opening price is, nonetheless, important and that it can be valuable in technical work.

Reconstructing the MATB using opening price as the determinant of moving average, let's examine some charts (Figures 15–10 and 15–11). Note the results. What is *most intriguing* to me about using the moving average of opening prices is the fact that the opening price is known early in each day's trading session. The MATB of opening prices is known when the markets open. Speculators could use the opening price as a means of calculating the MATB in order to forecast possible buy and sell points at support and resistance for use during the current day!

Consider the MATB in relation to the typical moving average work being done by most market technicians. I have also included

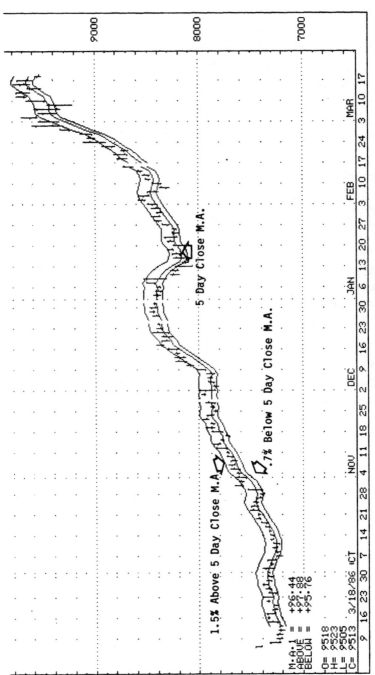

FIGURE 15–8: FIVE DAY CLOSE M.A. AND BAND
(Reprinted with Permission of Commodity Quote Graphics)

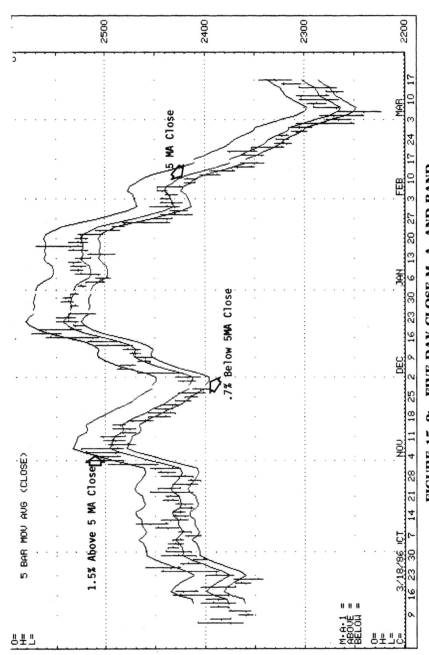

FIGURE 15-9: FIVE DAY CLOSE M. A. AND BAND
(Reprinted with Permission of Commodity Quote Graphics)

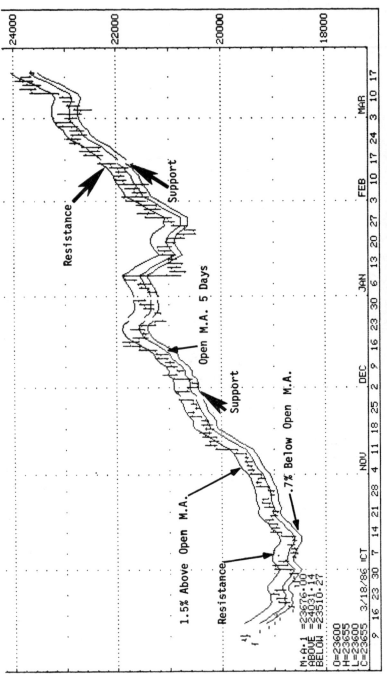

FIGURE 15–10: MOVING AVERAGE CHANNEL OPENING BAND
(Reprinted with Permission of Commodity Quote Graphics)

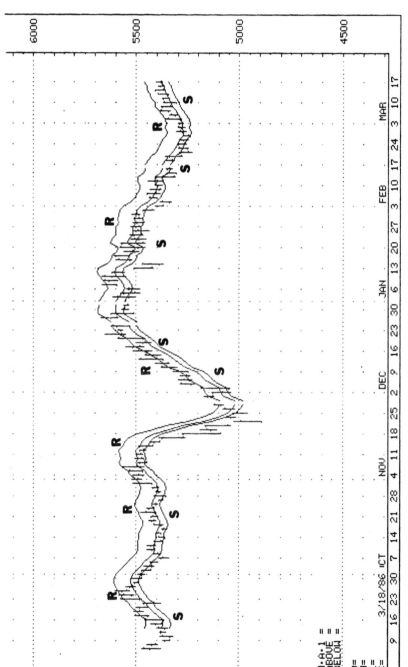

FIGURE 15–11: MOVING AVERAGE CHANNEL OPENING BAND

(R = RESISTANCE, S = SUPPORT)

(Reprinted with Permission of Commodity Quote Graphics)

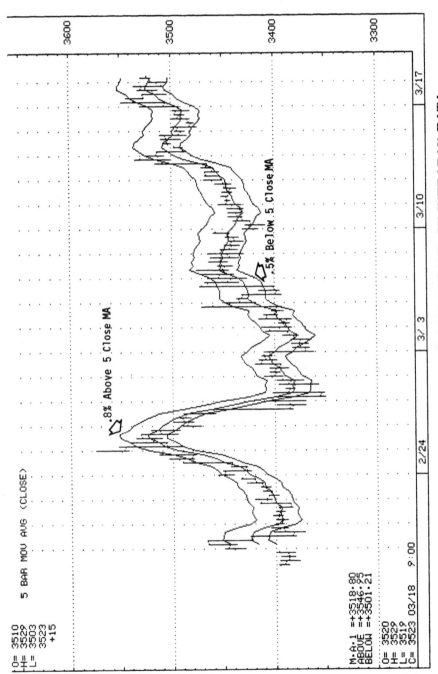

**FIGURE 15–12: MOVING AVERAGE TIMING BAND ON INTRADAY DATA
(Reprinted with Permission of Commodity Quote Graphics)**

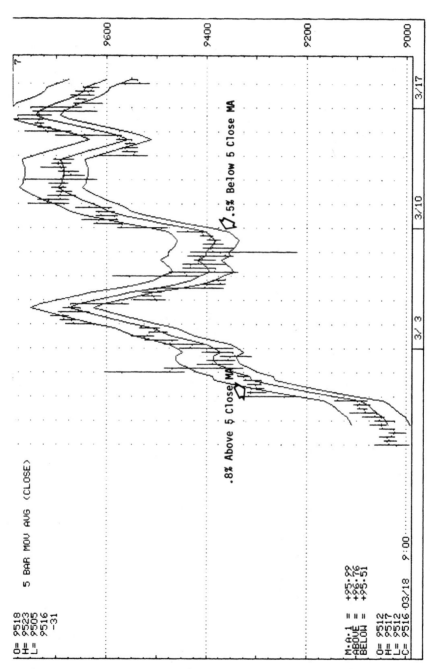

**FIGURE 15–13: MOVING AVERAGE TIMING BAND ON INTRADAY DATA
(Reprinted with Permission of Commodity Quote Graphics)**

SUMMARY

Two techniques for implementing moving averages were discussed. Both have good potential for development as trading systems. Particularly intriguing is the technique that employs opening prices, since opening prices are known early in the trading session and can be employed in a predictive fashion for the purpose of establishing support and resistance.

Chapter
16

Aspects of
Intraday Trading

For many years, futures traders and aspiring futures traders have been cautioned against the "evils of day trading." The public has been told that "day trading is for professionals, day trading is for floor traders, day trading is for speculators who are paying minimal commissions," and a host of other generalizations. Though it may have been true in the past that day trading was an art reserved only for the select few, a number of changes within the futures industry, as well as in the area of market technology, have significantly altered this situation.

Discount brokerage became popular in the 1980s, and the ensuing commission "price war" caused rates to fall precipitously. The competition has been fierce in the industry, but beneficial to the consumer. It has certainly taken its toll within the futures brokerage community.

Nonetheless, it now appears to me that the services many discount brokers provide are often equal to or better than what is true for many "full-service" firms. In view of the trend toward lower commission rates, increased computer power and the rapid communications now possible between the public speculator and the floor of the trading exchanges, intraday trading has become more of a reality for all types of traders. In the past we have been barraged by myriad reasons to avoid short-term trading. Now, however, it may be more reasonable to consider the possible benefits that may be derived from short-term trading.

Consider my list. It is not designed to influence you into making short-term or intraday trading your main focus, but rather to give you a different perspective from what you may have been exposed to in the past.

POSSIBLE ADVANTAGES OF INTRADAY TRADING

1. More efficient use of margin money.
2. Ability to test trading systems more rapidly in real time.
3. Intraday traders will need to do less market analysis, since they are not concerned with major price trends.
4. Intraday traders generally do not need to know the news since any intraday news will have an immediate impact on the market, thereby changing technical indicators, which, if reasonably good, will permit a capitalization on the trend change.
5. Intraday traders will be out of their positions at the end of the day win, lose or draw. An intraday trader who does not do so is not an intraday trader. Therefore, you will be forced to take your losses quickly, overcoming an obstacle that proves to be the undoing of many position traders (i.e., riding losses).
6. There are many good intraday price swings, particularly in the more active markets. This means that there is profit potential.
7. You will be forced to have discipline. Intraday trading requires the utmost discipline. It will be a good proving ground for you. Even if you choose not to do intraday trading consistently, the experience and the lessons learned will be valuable in all types of trading and investing.
8. You will obtain a fresh start each day. By starting fresh each day you will not be concerned about a loss or profit you may be riding from the previous day. The start of each new day is the start of a new relationship with the market, and with it a new opportunity.
9. You need not trade every day. Intraday traders can call it quits at the end of each day. Consequently, you can leave for trips,

vacations or other business any time you choose. You will not need to be concerned about a position you may have, and you will not need to be concerned about positions you may want to take.

There are probably many other potential advantages to intraday trading. Though this book is not intended to be a treatise in support of intraday trading, you may want to consider some of these advantages in your overall decision regarding the markets.

Certainly there are some prerequisites to intraday trading that must be met before a decision is made. Some of these have been discussed earlier in this book, but permit me to reiterate them as the major issues that face the individual who is about to make or has already made a decision to trade on an intraday basis. I would say that if you have any doubts about fulfilling all of the following prerequisites, then you ought not consider intraday trading.

PREREQUISITES TO INTRADAY TRADING

1. **Time**

   You must be able to make a time commitment. You must watch the market actively all day or until your positions have been closed out. You cannot do other things while trading intraday. You need not trade intraday every day of the week, but for those days that you do trade intraday, your total attention will be required.

2. **Quotes**

   In order to trade actively intraday, you will need one or all of the above. Some individuals believe that they can trade intraday using quotations obtained from television shows, radio talk commodity futures programs, or quotes from their broker. While it is possible to trade short term with limited information, intraday trading is either difficult or impossible if you do not have access to the above. While a computer itself may not be necessary, you must have a

method that is simple to calculate, permitting prompt decision making.

3. **Low Commissions**

Use a broker who charges you reasonably low commissions.
As I explained earlier, the cost of commissions is a major
one for the day trader. You must keep this cost as low as
possible, while retaining good price fills.

4. **Prompt Order Executions**

Frequently, you may be in and out of day trade positions
within a matter of minutes. If you should wish to exit a position within a matter of minutes after you entered, you will
need to know the price at which you entered. If you do
not know, then the delay of obtaining this information may
prove costly. This is why it is very important to trade with
a brokerage firm that can provide you with prompt reporting of order fills.

5. **Discipline**

I have already discussed the issue of discipline in this book.
I won't bother to underscore its importance in a day trading program. I refer you to previous chapters and sections
that deal with the subject.

6. **A Trading System or Method**

You will need a system that will alert you to intraday moves
very early in their inceptions.

These are some of the prerequisites to day trading. Review
them carefully. If you are currently day trading and find that your
results are not what they should be, or if you are considering day
trading, I urge you strongly to carefully consider the above.

OTHER ASPECTS OF INTRADAY TRADING

Another aspect of intraday trading is the issue of stop losses versus price objectives. The day trader must make decisions as to whether a position should be closed out once it reaches a certain profit objective, or whether a stop loss should be employed in the event that the position turns against the trader.

It is not an uncommon experience to have a position work in one's favor for a period of time, and then turn against one without a concomitant trading signal to change positions. On occasion, this will result in the profit being lost, and on some occasions the profit might actually turn into a loss. This is an unacceptable situation for the day trader, since profits must be closely guarded in order to preserve trading profitability on the bottom line. Two approaches can be used to solve this dilemma, each with its positive and negative aspects.

USING OBJECTIVES

One approach is to employ specific objectives for each market. In Treasury bonds, for instance, one might set an objective of 10 points. (This is merely an illustration. The 10-point objective is not something I have determined through research. I repeat, it is merely an illustration.) Every time the market allows you the opportunity to take a 10-point profit or greater, you will take it.

Unfortunately, the speculator who practices this approach may leave considerable profit in the market, should the position continue to move in the anticipated direction. Many times there are very large intraday moves and the practice of taking a 10-point profit will not only limit profits, but will also cause the speculator to lose his or her position. There may not be an opportunity to re-enter the market later in the day for participation in continued moves.

On the other hand, the market may reverse direction and the

speculator would be thankful that the 10-point profit was taken. Unfortunately there is no definitive way to know in advance what to do and when to do it. Therefore, an alternative procedure might be advisable.

TRAILING STOPS

Through the years there have been arguments both in favor of and opposed to trailing stops. Most of these discussions have been related to the use of stops for position trades. While it may be true that a trailing stop for position trades might not be an effective procedure, I maintain that a trailing stop should, indeed, be used for a day trade once a given profit objective has been attained. In other words, I recommend that once you have reached a certain profit level for each day trade (in dollar terms), you enter a stop loss that will pay your commissions and eliminate or greatly reduce the possibility of your profit turning into a loss. This will help avoid one of the worst situations for a day trader—allowing a profit to turn into a loss.

Furthermore, by a series of predetermined steps, the stop loss should be continually raised, closer and closer to the existing market price, so that as the day's end approaches, the possibility of locking in a profit is increased. Naturally, a level will be reached where it is absurd to place a stop loss and more advantageous to simply liquidate the position at the market.

SYSTEMS AND METHODS

The popularity of day trading and short-term trading is evidenced by the number of short-term trading systems that are available to the public. There are many different techniques for day trading, some employing "black box" systems whose details are not known to the user. Other technical systems which are available in the form of written computer software. Still other systems are less computerized or not computerized at all.

It is difficult to say which system or systems are best suited for use by any particular individual, since there are so many from which to choose and there are so many different objectives and expectations when it comes to intraday trading. Hopefully I can give you some guidelines and suggestions as to a few viable techniques.

"THE OLD STANDBYS"

Some of the traditional technical approaches described in this book are applicable to intraday trading. With the exception of the fact that all positions must be closed out by the end of the day's trading, the entry techniques discussed in this book are all reasonable methods. The exit techniques of such systems as moving averages, the moving average channel method, the moving average band method, traditional chart patterns and timing signal analysis are also viable. Futures traders, however, like all consumers, are always searching for the new and better, and in this search new products are constantly being developed for use by day traders.

Stop and consider, however, that the professional day trader on the floor of the exchange does not generally have access to a computer and must keep track of most technical work mentally or must trade on the basis of "gut feel." I certainly have nothing against trading on the basis of gut feel or intuition, as long as it is successful. Most individuals, however, cannot do this and, therefore, even trading in the pit requires some sort of a systematic approach, even if it is not as mechanical as might be desired.

As an addition to the standard techniques I have already described, all of which, to varying degrees can be applied to day trading, let me suggest to you an approach which until recently has not been especially practical since it requires constant monitoring of prices. It is, however, an approach for any individual who is in close touch with the markets.

The Tick Chart

The "tick chart" employs a very elementary concept. It is as elementary to use as it is to maintain. Yet, in its simplicity, it is highly complex since it represents a number of significant technical aspects of the market. The tick chart is, very simply, a price chart that records in dot fashion all prices at which a market trades during a given period of time. In other words, if one were recording a tick chart on gold futures using five-minute increments of time, one would simply place a dot (or some other distinguishing mark) at the appropriate coordinates on the chart in order to illustrate that the market had traded at that price.

That price, whatever it might have been, has already been "ticked at" and will not be recorded again. If the market were to continue to trade at that price, or if the market did not trade at all subsequent to this for the remainder of the five minutes, no other marks would be recorded in the five-minute time segment. When the five-minute segment ends, the next five-minute segment is started and a mark is placed at the next price tick. Assume that the market then ticks at a higher price. A tick is placed at that price. Assume then that the market ticks up again. A tick is placed in that price, and so on.

The method sounds simple enough. Yet, in its simplicity, it is most revealing. The tick chart allows the trader to determine levels of support, resistance, accumulation, distribution, breaks of resistance and breaks of support. By letting the trader know where and when considerable trading took place, the trader can have a good idea of where and when prices could find support on declines or resistance on rallies. The assumption is that if prices traded for a relatively long time within a given price range, then this level will likely serve as one of support when prices ultimately decline. Some of the other technical ramifications will be illustrated later on (See Figures 16–1 to 16–3).

The tick chart can be maintained on time frames of the user's choice. The shorter the time frame, the more active will be the trading signals generated by the tick chart. Furthermore, certain

Aspects of Intraday Trading

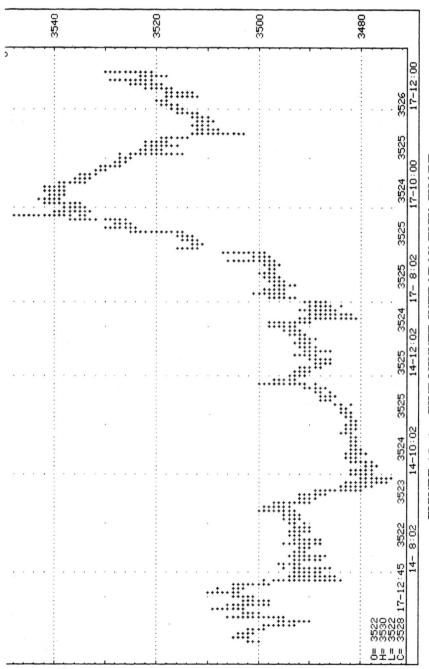

FIGURE 16–1: FIVE-MINUTE INTRADAY TICK CHART
(Reprinted with Permission of Commodity Quote Graphics)

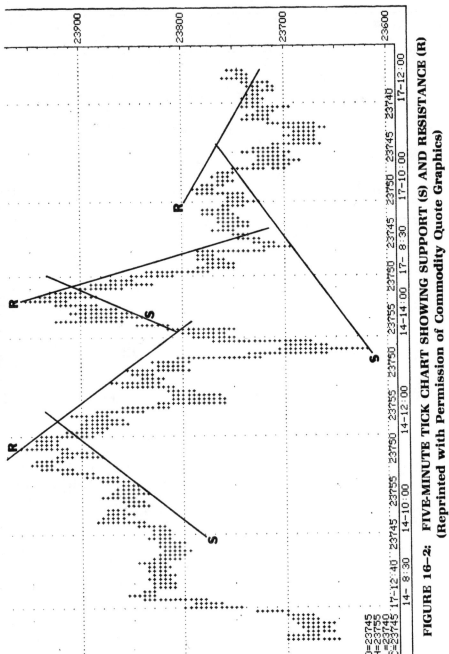

FIGURE 16–2: FIVE-MINUTE TICK CHART SHOWING SUPPORT (S) AND RESISTANCE (R)
(Reprinted with Permission of Commodity Quote Graphics)

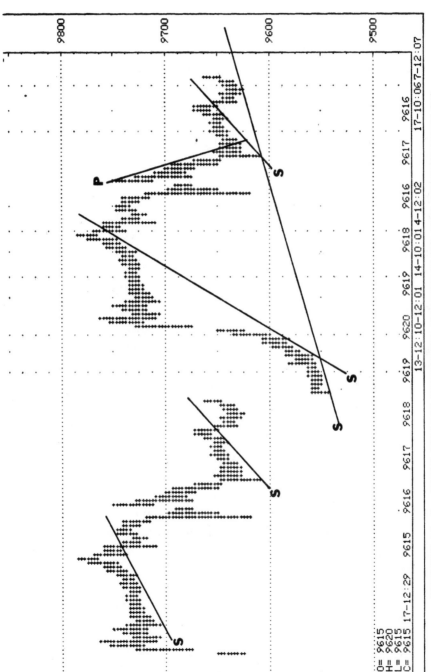

FIGURE 16–3: TICK CHART SHOWING SUPPORT (S) AND RESISTANCE (R)

(Reprinted with Permission of Commodity Quote Graphics)

forms of traditional analysis can be applied to the tick chart as means of generating additional signals.

In addition to the techniques described in this book, there are many other approaches, systems, methods and techniques to day trading. There are probably hundreds of different approaches, all of which may have potential, provided the basic rules of money management and sensibility are adhered to.

I can certainly say that with respect to intraday trading, discipline is more important than it is with any other approach. Yet, day trading has a built in disciplinarian, if you will, in the sense that the day trader must be out of his or her position at the end of the day if truly committed to day trading. I would say that with very few exceptions (probably fewer than five in 100) positions should never be kept overnight if you are strict about your day trading approach. All too often, those who do keep day trades overnight are rather disappointed they did so when the next day's trading begins.

This is not to say that significant amounts of money cannot be made by maintaining a position overnight, particularly in recent years, when opening price gaps have been particularly large. However, since the name of the day trading game is to reduce risk, why increase it by holding positions overnight?

SUMMARY

This chapter advanced the notion that intraday trading may not necessarily be the evil that so many have for so many years reported it to be. I outlined my reasons in favor of intraday trading, illustrated some intraday trading techniques, and also discussed what the prerequisites of intraday trading.

Chapter
17

Futures Options: Are They for You?

A more recent addition to the world of speculation is the futures option contract. Just as traders were beginning to understand stock indices, interest rate futures and currencies futures, along comes the futures options market to confuse the issue. It was rather ironic that futures options were unleashed upon the public during a period of time (1985–1986) that has been very difficult for many traders. Perhaps the rationale by those who have been planning futures options was to provide a vehicle to the public by which maximum loss would be the cost of the option plus commission.

To fully understand how options can be used and abused in futures trading, let's examine some very simple definitions of the futures options contract, and some elementary applications of these vehicles. Let me stress at the outset that this chapter *cannot in any way, shape or form, provide a comprehensive analysis and explanation of the literally hundreds of possible uses of futures options.* Interested parties should consult some of the recent texts on this subject. The discussion that follows should be sufficient to get you started in the right direction.

TWICE REMOVED

Futures options are very difficult for the average individual to understand because they deal with a "twice-removed" abstract concept. Stock options are simple to understand because they relate to an underlying security or a relatively tangible asset (i. e., shares of stock, which represent ownership of an entity). An option on a future is, in effect, an intangible on top of an intangible. Since a futures contract often represents something that has not yet been produced or manufactured, an option to buy or sell something that is not yet real is even more abstract to the general public.

Yet, the concept should not be so unfamiliar, since many areas of the investor's world currently deal in fairly similar abstracts. Options on new construction are a good example. A builder begins to develop a piece of property for apartments or condominiums. In order to sell the units, the builder sells options to buy units that have not yet been constructed. The option gives a buyer the right to purchase one of the units by a certain date. Sale of the option raises cash for the builder and locks in the buyers right to purchase a unit (usually at a fixed price) at some point in the future, regardless of what prices may have risen to or fallen to by that time. The buyer of the real-estate option can apply the purchase price toward the purchase of the unit at contract closing.

In many ways, the futures option is similar, but the buyer won't necessarily get his or her money back when the contract expires. A futures option gives the buyer of the option the right to buy or sell the underlying futures contract at a given price at some time in the future, regardless what the actual price may be. Therefore, if a buyer of an option is fortunate, or better yet, has done good technical research on exercised good judgment, and the underlying market moves in his or her favor, the option will increase in value, since the underlying futures contract will increase in value.

The creators of futures options, in their great wisdom and foresight, have given us two types of options. The call option gives the buyer the right to buy the underlying futures contract by a certain date at a certain price regardless of the actual price. The put option gives its buyer the right to sell the futures contract at a certain price at some point in the future regardless of what the actual price may be. You can readily see that if you buy a call option and the price of the underlying commodity goes up, you make money. If you buy a put option and the price of the underlying commodity goes down you also make money. There is certainly no more mystery to this than being long or short the market.

MANY WAYS TO GO

Imagine the myriad possibilities that are feasible when futures and options are employed in conjunction. The many different combinations or strategies include such things as buying a call option and selling a call option of a different month, buying a call option and buying a put option at the same time, buying the underlying commodity and buying the put option to protect yourself, buying call options instead of the underlying commodity to minimize risk, buying put options instead of the underlying commodity to minimize risk, and so on. There are numerous combinations of the above.

Is it no wonder then, that options and option strategies have proven overwhelming to most speculators. Due to such complexities, their reception into the world of futures trading has not been an especially smooth one, with the exception of options on Treasury bond futures. Primarily this poor reception has been a function of ignorance on the part of the public and its consequent unwillingness to accept futures options as a viable means of limiting risk.

ADVANTAGES OF FUTURES OPTIONS

The advertised advantage of futures options is the fact that their buyers have limited risk. Risk is limited to the cost of the option plus commission. In other words, if purchase of a futures options contract costs you $600, then the absolute maximum you can lose will be commission plus $600. Such limited loss factor has great appeal to the public and constitutes the primary marketing tool used to interest speculators in futures options.

A secondary benefit of options is the fact that they can increase tremendously on a percentage basis over a very short period of time. Couple this with specific limited loss and tremendous upside potential, and you have an almost ideal situation on which to "sell" a speculator.

Another benefit of futures options is that, up to a certain point in time, they will continue to hold their value and, as a consequence, they will buy you time without forcing you out of the market. If, for example, you expect gold to make a major move down, but you do not know for certain when the move will occur, you could buy a put option without being concerned that you must have precise timing on your entry. The put will buy you time and, within a reasonable time frame, you will be able to withstand moves in the market against you knowing that your maximum loss is specifically limited. The only way you can lose is if the market continues to go against you or if the market goes nowhere.

This "buying time" feature is specially beneficial to a agricultural producer who may wish to hedge against crops by purchasing the appropriate put options. Since the market for many options is large and liquid, he could close out the option at any time. Naturally, however, the worst thing that can happen is that your option will become worthless and you will lose its entire value.

Another feature of options is that their value can be very accurately predicted at any point in time. Each option's value is clearly related to the underlying value of the futures contract it represents and its time to expiration. A considerable number of statistical computer programs are available in the field of options evaluation. These programs will allow you to evaluate various strategies over a specific period of time, using possible price objectives. They will give you the potential value of your option, given the outcome of each scenario. Institutional money managers, stock fund managers and pension fund managers can employ options in stock index futures and Treasury bond future, in programs to hedge against their holdings either in the cash markets and/or in stocks/mutual funds.

LIABILITIES AND LIMITATIONS OF FUTURES OPTIONS

The single greatest liability of futures options is that they provide speculators with a false sense of security. Whereas the producer may certainly benefit the public or individual speculator frequently feels that he or she is taking less risk in entering an options position than might be taken in entering the futures market. The speculator may be enticed out of making a trade in the net market, since he or she feels that an option will cost less and could yield more.

While it is true that the option may indeed cost less and could yield more, it appears just as difficult to make money speculating in options as it does speculating in futures. The logic of options seems to be irrefutable, but it must be fully understood that time is of the essence. The speculator reasons, "Why should I risk losing $1600 in gold on a futures contract when I can buy a gold call option for $850, with the possibility that gold may rally several thousand dollars per contract?" The hope or expectation here is that the individual will have sufficient time to participate in at least a portion of the move. Had a position been taken in nothing but the futures contract, it is possible that the trader may not have been able to withstand a move in the opposite direction. But the option also had limited time.

The use of a limited-risk futures options strategy in conjunction with cyclic price tendencies is a very sensible strategy. The procedure is described at the end of this chapter in greater detail. Though options will limit your risk, you may take many more total losses due to deterioration of time value (called "time decay").

ARE FUTURES OPTIONS FOR YOU?

The attractiveness of futures options due to their limited risk and high profit potential can be illusory. The speculator should not only see the limited risk and high potential, but he or she should also be aware of the downside. If 20 option positions are taken with a loss of $400 on most, then the few winners must be large ones if the overall result is to be positive. Although you may be enamored of the obvious benefits in options, you should not lose sight of their probability of success when used in the typical fashion. Certainly, if this is your first venture into the futures trading area, and if you have very limited capital, then options may not be the right thing for you.

The specific manner in which you use futures option strategies is significantly more important than the underlying limited risk of these vehicles. As in the case of futures market transactions, you must attempt to use options in the same way that professionals do. This is not especially simple, but there are very specific methods and procedures for doing so.

As you can see, futures options are for you if you use them the right way. If, however, you are looking to make a killing by trading extremely low priced (i. e., out of the money) futures options, then your odds are not especially good. I will assume that you have some very general knowledge of options trading, since my purpose in this book is not to cover the field of options from start to finish. The intent is, as I have expressed earlier, to give a very general overview that will ultimately provide you with direction and save you time. Remember, above all, that futures options trading is not a panacea for avoiding losses.

SOME SUGGESTED STRATEGIES

Here are some very elementary strategies that are feasible, but that, as you will see, have different applications. I suggest you should consult a more thorough text for complete strategic methodology if you have a serious interest in futures options implementation.

1. **Buy a Call Option Instead of Going Long**
   Assume that you have good reason to believe that a market is going higher. You wish to limit your risk by using an option instead of buying the underlying futures contract. What should you do? Here are a few questions to consider. Do you expect a large move or a small move? Do you expect a short-term move or a long-term move? How much time should it take?

   Generally, if you expect a short-term move, then you might consider buying an in-the-money option or an option that is near the money. In other words, an in-the-money option is one that trades above the strike price, whereas a near-the-money option is one that trades close to the strike price. Such options will be higher priced, but they will move at the same rate or at a greater rate than the underlying market.

   An alternate procedure that involves lower risk would be to buy options that are farther from the money by virtue of their nearer expiration or larger distance from the strike price. Such options may be selling at much lower prices, but may only move one-third as quickly as the underlying contract. In order to answer these types of questions, it is best to use an options evaluation program—either one provided by a software service or one maintained by your brokerage house. You can get some very specific answers to these questions by running an evaluation program.

2. **Buy Put Options in Expectation of a Down-Move**
   The procedure here would be essentially similar to what has been described for call options above, but you would buy puts instead of calls expecting price to move lower, and the puts to move up. The same general rules would apply.

3. **You Expect a Large Up-Move; Buy Futures and Buy Put Options for Protection**
   To a certain extent, this is a spread strategy. Assume that you expect a market to move much higher and you plan on

purchasing, or you have already purchased, a net long position in the futures market. Assume also that you wish to protect yourself from having a naked long position or assume you want to protect your call option. You could get some protection by buying a put option that would be limited in cost, but, in the event of a decline in your underlying long position, would protect you from significant loss.

Naturally, you would be liable for commissions on each, and if your net long position goes in your favor, the put option position will decrease in value. This, however, is not an especially bad strategy since there is no limit to how high the long futures contract may go, but the put option can only decrease to zero. If, for example, you establish a long position in soybeans expecting a 50-cent up-move (which would be worth $2,500 per contract) and you establish a long put option position (costing you $700), your potential would be $2,500 minus $700 worth of "insurance."

Assuming that the long soybeans went against you, your put option would increase in value, though not necessarily on a par with the decrease in value of your long position. The right combination of long futures and long put options is necessary to give you complete protection. Remember that "time decay" is your enemy.

4. **Sell Short Futures; Buy a Call for Protection**
   This procedure works exactly the opposite way from the one just described. Again, the right fit or match of call options and short futures contracts is important for complete protection.

5. **You Expect a Major Move, but You Don't Know which Way**
   Some markets are notorious for making big moves. Treasury bond futures, for example, has made some major moves through the years. Yet there are times when you are not certain which way the move will go. Underlying

market conditions such as bullish consensus, trading volume, economic factors, chart patterns, cycles, volumes, etc., all suggest that the market is likely to make a large move. Still, you are not certain in which direction. You could purchase a put and a call on the same market, which would mean that the only way you would come out at a loss is if this market fails to make a big move during this life span of your options.

6. **Covered Options Strategies Are Also Possible**
   In such cases, you become the seller of a call or put option, taking in the money from the buyer and protecting yourself with a futures position that will cover you in the event of a move against you. These strategies are considerably safer, yet they may not yield as much as naked options sales.

7. **Differential in Long-Term, Short-Term and Intermediate-Term Moves**
   Many times, the market will move differently based on near-term and far-term expectations. A prime example is short-term and long-term interest rates. While there are times that short-term interest rates will decline with long-term interest rates holding steady, there may also be times in during which long-term interest rates decline and short-term rates actually go up. Such situations are ideal for spreading two ends against this middle or various combinations of spreads.

   Such spreads using futures options are numerous, and an entire science of spreading with its own lingo and methodology has evolved in recent years. The simple act of spreading near-term vs long-term vs midterm rates is called a butterfly spread. In such an instance, a speculator might buy a nearby option, buy a deferred option, and sell two options in the middle. Such spreads can combine exceptionally low risk with tremendous profit potential, provided your timing and conceptualization of market conditions are correct. For those wishing to dig more deeply into this subject, there are many good references available.

SUMMARY

This overview clarified the doubly intangible nature of futures options. Many distinct strategies employing futures options were identified and later discussed, especially regarding their value in limiting speculators' and producers' risks. Readers were warned against the limitations inherent in trading futures options, including limited profit potential as compared to the underlying futures contracts. Time decay, or the rapid time deterioration of the options premium was mentioned as a severely negative factor.

Chapter

18

How to Develop Your Own Trading Plan

Whereas the futures trader of yesteryear suffered from a dearth of technical information, today's futures trader frequently suffers from information overload. A common complaint I hear from many futures traders, both in the public and professional sectors, is that there is too much information to digest. There are literally hundreds of trading systems) perhaps thousands of different trading techniques and many different computer software programs, computer hardware combinations, etc. There are countless newsletter services, chart services, advisors, consultants, brokers, managed-account programs, guided-account programs, pools, etc. In addition to the above, futures trading has now been complicated by the addition of many new futures contracts as well as futures options. Even veteran traders can find themselves overwhelmed.

Many of us are beginning to question the value of the time-tested approaches and the markets. We have seen trading volume in the agricultural futures markets decline while volume in the financially related markets has soared. As an aside, it is interesting to note that the switch has been from the basic, or "tangible," commodities to the intangible commodities (i.e., interest rates, stock indices, currencies). This is, no doubt, an expression of the current state of world affairs, but it is, nonetheless, a reality with which all traders, veteran and novice, must contend.

Given the over-supply of information and the difficulty many traders encounter in formulating an overall trading plan, this chapter will attempt to simplify the process for you by pointing out some factors that will naturally limit your choices. Remember that the term "trading plan" does not refer to a specific system, method or technique. It refers to an overall approach that covers virtually every aspect of the trader and the market from psychology to finances. The term "trading plan" is a global term. When you are done with this chapter, you should be able to take the many different aspects of the entire book and turn them into a workable program that will, hopefully, help you accomplish many of your goals and objectives in the most efficient, enjoyable and relatively painless fashion.

BEGIN BY LISTING YOUR LIMITATIONS

The problem most aspiring traders encounter when initiating a trading plan is that they attempt to reach for heights that are, in reality, unattainable. Though their goals may seem simple enough, the reality of the situation is that many goals cannot be attained due to limitations on the part of the trader or speculator. It is unrealistic, for example, to expect that you might continue your present occupation full-time while also attempting to successfully day trade the futures markets.

We have been told for many years that we must set our sights high if we wish to achieve great things. This may very well be true, yet to set goals high without allowing for the raw materials that will make the goals attainable is to guarantee frustration and failure. I would, therefore, suggest that your first task in forming a trading plan be to list your specific limitations, as opposed to listing your specific goals. Your goals will be directly determined and limited by the amount of input you can give to fulfilling these goals.

It's time to make a list again! And it will be wise to check it more than twice. Your list should begin with a specific indication of how much time you have each day and/or week to give to the markets. You should also list precisely when you can give this time each day. Time given to the market after trading hours is distinctly different than time that can be given during the day. Among the items your list might include are the following:

1. How much time can you give the market each day (week)?
2. If you can devote time each day, then is this time you will give during market hours or after market hours?
3. Do you want to buy a computer?
4. Do you want to pay for a tick-by-tick quote service?
5. How much of what you want to have (i.e., as above in items 3 and 4) is covered in the money you have allocated to trading?
6. Do you want to spend time each day watching the market, or actively trading a specific system? If so, how much time can you give?
7. Are you willing and able to take the pressure of intraday trading?
8. Are you willing to ride large losses, or are you willing to take small but more frequent losses at the worst?

Many other factors, some general, some individual, should be considered as part of your list. The essence of the list is that it will limit you what you can realistically attempt. This is why all trading plans must begin with your limitations.

NOW, LIST YOUR GOALS

For most traders, the goals will be financial. If so, then list them in terms of dollars or in terms of percent return on starting capital. Once these goals have been listed, *re-examine them in the light of your limitations.* This will give you a very good idea if your goals are realistic in terms of your limitations. If you realize now that your expectations cannot become realities within the limits of your time, finances, etc., then change your goals to be in closer accord with your limitations.

You may need to go through this process several times until you have finally arrived at a workable combination. Your efforts should be directed toward setting goals that are attainable. Also, make certain that you set a reasonable time limit within which the goals can be achieved.

THE IMPORTANCE OF BEING REALISTIC

At this juncture I want to emphasize the importance of being realistic in all of your dealings with the markets. Inasmuch as there many stories of fabulous success in the marketplace, the speculator is often tempted to believe that such success may be achieved with limited effort. While it is certainly true that some individuals acquire vast fortunes in futures trading beginning with virtually nothing and within a very limited time, this is clearly the exception rather than the rule. To believe that you can achieve such results is not realistic. Your chances are about as good as those of winning one of the state lotteries. If part of your trading plan includes achievement of such a goal beginning with minimal capital, limited time input and over a brief period of time, then you are most certainly fooling yourself. While it is not my intent to discourage creative and motivating dreams, it is indeed my intention to discourage virtually all traces of unrealistic fantasy when it comes to success in futures trading.

If you begin your relationship with the market (or if you maintain your relationship with the market) by dealing in irrational fantasies and expectations you will be prone to use wishful thinking in other areas of the relationship, as well. As an example, consider the wishful thinking which prompts traders to hold on to a losing position well past their stop loss point. Consider the wishful thinking that prompts traders to hold on to winning positions well past their objectives, often watching a good profit turn into a loss. This is the kind of thinking that will be stimulated by unrealistic goals. Your relationship must be the *single most honest* relationship of your life. It requires being honest with yourself. You cannot fool the market, you can only fool *yourself.*

Virtually every unrealistic fantasy and action in the markets will come back to haunt you, perhaps for a long time. Hence, my very stern admonition to avoid all unrealistic expectations and fantasies when you create your trading plan, and, above all, when you put it into action!

NOW DECIDE ON YOUR TRADING APPROACH

The general aspects of different trading approaches, systems and methods are given in this book. As I have indicated, my coverage of these is very general. Once you've decided that a given approach is best suited to you within the constraints already outlined in this chapter, then acquire more information. If you're an experienced trader already employing a given approach, then take the time to re-evaluate it in terms of the guidelines provided in this chapter. You may find that what you've been doing for a long time is really not for you! you may find that a totally different approach is best suited to your other needs and limitations.

The approach, system or method you use need not be complicated, sophisticated, computer generated or mystical. All you need is a method by which you can generate the following:

1. Entry and exit signals that have a record of accuracy in excess of 65–75 percent,
2. Specific method of entry and exit, once signals have been generated,
3. Specific objective or reversing point,
4. Specific money management of signals such as a stop loss, dollar risk amount, reversing point, etc., and
5. A system that does not have periods of severe drawdown.

This last issue, "drawdown," is an important one to consider in evaluating any trading system or approach.

THE IMPORTANCE OF UNDERSTANDING "DRAWDOWN"

The hypothetical trading results of many systems are absolutely incredible when taken over a period of many years and when examined on the bottom line. Yet, when studied in detail, some of these systems would have required sitting through periods of severe reversals in total profit. If you had started trading such a system near a peak or just prior to a period of severe drawdown, you would have had to suffer through a period of persistent losses.

Such losses might not only cause you personal and emotional anguish, but they could easily deplete all of your risk capital, knocking you out of the game before the system recouped its losses and went on to score major gains. Since your market entry is, in some respects, a random event, you may not be astute enough to enter at the most propitious time, therefore, opening yourself to the possibility of a severe drawdown. There are a number of very cogent ways to avoid such a situation. Here are a few significant strategies for avoiding of drawdown.

1. Select systems that have shown minimal drawdown. You may have to sacrifice total performance for minimal drawdown, but it's a good tradeoff.
2. Remember that a good record of limited drawdown in the past is no guarantee of minimal drawdown in the future, but it can help you decide.
3. Begin trading a given system only after a period of drawdown. This may require you to wait a while before you begin trading a given system, but you will be less apt to be starting at the wrong time and you may have to sit through less of a move against you.

The last suggestion is the most important. To wait and act only after a period of drawdown would be similar to waiting for a good investment to decline in value so that you can enter on a setback thereby reducing overall risk.

WHEN YOU EVALUATE A TRACK RECORD . . .

In formulating your trading plan, you will want to select or create a system or method that best suits your needs. One of the key considerations is the performance history of the given system or method. The hypothetical (and even real-time) trading record is one of the most misunderstood things in the world of futures trading. There are so many things to remember about track records that I can't possibly cover all of them. I can, however, give you some points I consider exceptionally important to all who are considering a given system. This holds true whether you are buying a given trading system or whether you have created your own system. Please note the following vital issues!

1. Determine the maximum margin required to follow all trades and calculate this in addition to the drawdown of the system. It may take some time to figure, but it will be well worthwhile! By knowing the absolute worst case historically, you will have, at the very minimum, an idea of how bad things have gotten.

2. Take commission costs into consideration. Some hypothetical performance records *do not show commission costs as losses.* The cost of commissions can certainly add up. Don't forget to take these into consideration, or to recalculate the results to reflect the commissions you are paying.

3. Some performance records base profits on the purchase and sale of multiple contracts in different contract months for the same market. In other words, a system may buy or sell several different contract months in a given market at the same time. This tends to weight the profitable side of the record, often quite substantially. Be aware of this when you evaluate a record.

4. Beware of track records that have a limited history! You can prove virtually anything if your statistics are manipulated in the right way. Some trading systems show fantastic results over the last five years, yet prior to this the systems did not work well at all. Some systems work exceptionally well in bull or bear markets, but fail miserably in sideways markets. A thorough system test should include samples of performance in classic bull markets, bear markets and sideways markets.

5. Spot check hypothetical price fills. They may assume a much better price fill than might have been possible in real time. Ideally, a system test should give the worst possible alternatives, not the best.
6. Determine how money management is used as part of the system. Is the system a reversing one, or are specific stops used with each trade? This is important since it will give you an indication of how trades are closed out. When evaluating stops and risks, take into consideration your personal and financial abilities.

There are many other issues to consider, but I have given you highlights of those that I believe deserve maximum attention.

PLAN YOUR TIME/MAKE A SCHEDULE

Once you've made all of the major decisions, it will be time to put these decisions into practice. The best way to ruin a good trading system and good intentions is to implement them in an inconsistent or disorganized fashion. In order to utilize your time, money, and systems in the most efficient and effective way possible, you must make yourself a schedule. Your schedule should be precise. It should detail what you plan to do, how, when and for how long. You should schedule your time and you should then follow the schedule.

It is only when you implement your plans in real time that you will be able to work out any details, limitations or problems that you have not considered in your planning. Once you have found the schedule that works best for you, stick to it. You will know how well your schedule is working for you by your performance in the markets.

EVALUATE PROGRESS REGULARLY

Last, but certainly not least, it is important to continually evaluate the progress of your trading plan. The ultimate measure of the plan will be your performance in the markets. However, performance itself will not tell you precisely where you have been strong or weak in your application of the rules and procedures. For this reason, you must constantly monitor your performance and implementation of the trading plan. Refer back to your list of trades frequently and study the reasons for your profits and losses. This list will, I believe, be the single most valuable source of educational feedback you will have at your disposal. If you keep it up to date and if you are totally honest in your record keeping, then you will benefit greatly.

SUMMARY

This chapter gave specific suggestions regarding the formulation of a trading plan. Emphasis was placed upon analysis of performance records, organization and accurate record keeping.

Chapter
19

How to Learn from Your Losses

The cost of education is high. In futures trading it is higher than in virtually any other venture. The cost is measured not only in dollars, but in emotion as well. In view of the tremendous outlay, both financial and personal, that is required to learn futures trading, it is imperative to make each and every loss a lesson in more effective trading. In other words, each loss much be used to its utmost as a learning experience. Since you will want to learn the art and science of futures speculation as quickly and as efficiently as possible, it is necessary to take advantage of each and every experience with the markets, good and bad.

Learning psychologists know that all organisms can learn from positive, as well as from negative experiences. They also know that it is often more difficult to learn from negative experiences than it is from positive ones. This is due to the simple fact that there are literally thousands of things you can do wrong, but only a few things you can do right. Therefore, if you are punished (i.e., by taking a loss in the market) each time you do something wrong, you won't necessarily learn anything from it. It will only tell you what not to do the next time. It won't, however, tell you what the right behavior may be. Similarly, a reward for the "wrong" behavior will also prove counterproductive.

Since most trades in the futures markets are closed out as losses, we've must use losses as a learning tool. Though this is not the ideal situation, the market is not a patient teacher. In fact, the market is a terrible teacher. Sometimes the market will reward you for doing the wrong thing and sometimes it will punish you for doing the right thing. As you can easily see, the marketplace is a difficult environment in which to learn. We must, therefore, take matters into our own hands and do the best we can with what we have. We must make the most of the market feedback we get. This feedback, the "raw material" of our learning, consists primarily of losses, but to some extent, of profits as well.

What I propose to do in this chapter is to give you some guidelines by which you can structure your learning situation. This chapter will provide you with a general framework within which to evaluate your losses, but it will also help you understand your profits. If you are convinced, as I am, that learning is the key to behavior, then you will quickly grasp the importance of viewing losses and profits in an analytical way.

Perhaps this chapter would have been better titled "How to Learn from Profits and Losses," but as a matter of fact, it's much more simple to learn from profits. This is why my focus will be primarily upon learning from losses. I will mention a number of items in connection with learning from profits.

WHEN YOU MAKE A TRADE/
WHEN YOU CLOSE OUT A TRADE

The first important bit of advice I can give regarding losses and profits is to keep a record of all trades. Rather than just a record of entry and exit prices, dates, profits and losses, which most traders keep, the record keeping system I propose is much more detailed. I suggest you keep the following information on every single trade.

1. **Entry and Exit Date, Entry and Exit Prices**
   This is, of course, standard procedure.

2. **Reason for Making the Trade**
   This is a very important aspect of the record keeping approach. By forcing yourself to list the reason(s) for each and every trade, you will be forced to stick to your trading system rules. You will avoid the temptation of making trades on whims, tips or inside information. You'll avoid the temptation to jump into and out of trades based on factors which are not related to your trading system or method. In other words, *before you act,* you'll need to know why! This will help cut down on many impulsive trades that, in the long run, are losing trades.

   By adding this simple requirement to your record-keeping system you will help avoid mistakes. In addition, you will have a permanent record of why each trade was made. If you entered the trade within the parameters of your system or method and ended up taking a loss, you'll be able to go back over the record in order to evaluate your decision. Perhaps you made a mistake in understanding your indicators or signals. If you rely entirely on memory, the reasons will be lost in the shuffle.

3. **Reason for Closing out Position**
   This is just as important as point 2. This will help you pinpoint the exact reasoning you employed in closing out a trade. Many traders can enter a trade for the right reasons, but they go astray when it comes to closing out trades. They tend to become emotional once in a trade. Emotion can cause them to either stay too long, riding a loss, or to get out too soon, taking a profit that might have been much larger in the long run. Therefore, make certain you keep a thorough record of why trades were closed out.

4. **Reason for Profit or Loss**

By studying or analyzing the reasons for your profits or losses (as indicated by items 2 and 3), you will be able to analyze what you are doing right and what you are doing wrong. Generally, you will see that the reasons for your losses tend to cluster around the same types of errors. These will, most often, be emotional as opposed to technical. With most trading systems you'll take as many as 6–8 losses out of 10 trades due to the nature of trading systems. However, if you're taking 8 or more losses out of 10 trades, and if the reasons are not directly due to the system error rate itself, then you will know very quickly by examining your record.

STUDY THE RECORD REGULARLY

Once you have mastered the record keeping aspect, use the record to learn! This means that you will need to study the record regularly. If you're an active trader, then study the record at the end of every trading day and review your learning the next morning before the markets open. If you are not an active trader, then once weekly will be sufficient.

I strongly urge you to *understand each and every loss* and not to trade again until you do. If you study the record and force yourself to learn from it, then your losses will truly help you grow. Failure to employ losses in the fashion I have outlined means that you are not using your tuition wisely.

Furthermore, by studying your losses, you will be able to determine very quickly what has gone wrong. You can decide if errors were trader errors, system errors, broker errors, etc. You will know very quickly if your trading system is at fault. If this is clearly the case, then you will be able to change systems. If, on the other hand, you find that you are at fault, you will be able to take the action required to make the changes, as well.

PROFITS CAN HELP YOU LEARN AS WELL

In your quest for reasons and explanations and in your efforts to learn, don't overlook the importance of learning from profits, as well. A profit will let you know when you've done something correctly, but don't be fooled into thinking that profits can only come from correct action. At times, the market will generate a profit whether or not you acted correctly. The market is not entirely consistent. If the market was a bastion of consistency, then there would be no reason for writing this book.

Be very careful about profits that come after a behavior that was not appropriate. In other words, assume that you did something incorrect, but that you were rewarded with a profit. This is a potentially dangerous situation since you may be exposed to bad learning. The profit will reward you for doing something that was not consistent with your system or with effective trading behavior.

If you find that your application of trading rules and principles is resulting in profits most of the time, then you are on the right track and you should stay on it!

REMEMBER TO BE CONSISTENT

Whatever you do, remember that consistency is very important in the effective use of trading losses as a vehicle to improve learning. Many individuals begin their record-keeping system with excellent intentions, but they tend to go astray and, in the long run, their good intentions are worthless. If you begin the process of tracking your trading and evaluating your profits and losses, then by all means continue it to its logical conclusion.

All too often, traders tend to abandon their lists when the going gets tough. They let losses demoralize them. Once this happens, you will no longer learn from your losses. They will not serve you as a means to facilitate learning. Instead, you will learn nothing and you will not benefit in any way, shape or form. Eventually you will be forced out of the market and when you re-enter at some later point with more capital, you will make the same mistakes again.

LOSSES AND BEHAVIORS TEND TO REPEAT

Losses and behaviors work in patterns. The patterns tend to repeat. Very often, behavior will cluster into certain types or groups. Some traders make most of their mistakes by being impatient, and other traders make most of their mistakes by not taking losses. There are, in fact, so many different things a speculator can do wrong that it is virtually useless to try and find each and every one of them.

If you know that behaviors tend to repeat, if you know where you tend to make most of your errors, and if you know that whether your errors are due to your system or yourself, you will have at least half the battle won. When you analyze your results, remember to look for patterns in your trading losses. I am certain you will find these patterns. Furthermore, I am certain that once you find them, you will discover that there are some very simple ways in which to overcome the errors and, thereby, to reduce the losses. Many of these have already been discussed in this book.

LEARN TO STAND ASIDE IF YOU DON'T UNDERSTAND

Many traders feel that they must be in the markets at all times. Nothing could be more inaccurate. If you have done a good job with your record keeping, if you have been consistent with your application of the trading rules and if you have done your best to learn from you losses, but if you are still confused or uncertain as to why you are taking losses, then stand aside. Perhaps the best way to avoid repeating errors is to stand aside until you understand them. Some traders would disagree with this reasoning.

While it may be true that a seasoned veteran of trading need not stand aside, the newcomer cannot trade without understanding. While the "old timer" may have a better grasp of the ups and downs of trading, knowing when he or she has reached the limit, the newcomer does not have such knowledge and must learn from the very start.

HOW TO IMPLEMENT YOUR LEARNING

The best way to put learning into action is by making a list of what your findings have been and by putting the list into action. Let's assume that you have your list. Let's also assume that there are about five major items on your list. The way to begin putting your knowledge into practice is by referring to the list every time you enter or exit a trade to make certain you are not making one of the targeted errors. This is a very simple process. It is strictly mechanical and it should not pose a serious problem to anyone seriously interested in changing his or her results in a beneficial way.

CONTINUE TO MONITOR RESULTS

Do not abandon your list once you have isolated the problem areas. Your record-keeping system will be important to you in providing ongoing feedback. If you continue to track your results and performance, you will know when you are beginning to make mistakes and you will be able to end them quickly. Remember that not all losses in the markets are due to your behavior. It is very possible that you'll find your system is at fault after you begin to track your performance and behaviors. Unless you implement the suggestions I have given you, it will be difficult for you to know precisely what is at fault.

KNOW YOUR WEAKNESSES AND STRENGTHS

Another aspect of learning from losses is that you will know your weaknesses and strengths. By knowing when and how you make mistakes, you will be able to avoid getting into situations that may cause you to act incorrectly. By knowing your strengths, you will be able to take advantage of situations that are tailor made to your skills. As you can see, the purpose of record keeping is many fold, and its potential advantages make the effort well worthwhile.

DON'T TAKE LOSSES PERSONALLY

There is no doubt that losses are painful. Every loss hurts, but it can hurt more if your attitude toward losses is a negative one. If you look upon each loss as an opportunity to learn, and if you look upon your initial risk capital as tuition, expecting to lose most of it, your attitude toward losses will be a positive one. This does not mean that you'll learn to love losses. It does, however, mean that each loss can lead to new learning.

If do not take each loss as a personal defeat, then you will not allow losses to negatively affect your behaviors in the market. Your approach to futures trading should be similar to the approach of any individual entering a new business. You must take about a year to learn the business, and you must not expect your first year to be a winning one.

Futures trading appears to take longer to learn any other business I know. The process can be a very slow one indeed. As a matter of fact, the learning process in futures trading never stops. There are always lessons to learn. Hopefully, with the passage of time, the losses will become less frequent and the lessons will not have to be learned over and over again, but all of this can only be achieved if you have the proper attitude toward losses. As I stated earlier, you must have, or you must develop, the proper attitude toward losses. Failure to do so will likely inhibit the learning process.

YOUR EGO, COMPETITION AND LOSSES

It has been said that competition is a healthy thing. While this may be true for the professional athlete, it is not necessarily true for the futures trader. In sports, you know who it is that you are competing against. In the futures market, however, you do not know your foe. If you envision your rival to be the entire market, then you have set yourself an impossible task, since you will never defeat the entire market.

Who, then, should your competitor be? I maintain that you must always compete with yourself. Do not look at what other traders have done. Do not attempt to overcome their success. Don't set your standards so terribly high that you will never be able to achieve them. The market holds a vast treasure with sufficient wealth for many traders. Naturally, not all traders can be winners. Losers must feed the pot, but the rational futures trader will seek to dip into the pot for only a small portion of its immense wealth.

You must always be your own chief rival. Compete with your own results. Try to better your own record. There will always be someone who claims to be doing better than you are. This should be of no consequence to you.

The ego of a trader is very important. There are literally hundreds of potentially ego-deflating experiences the market can unleash upon the trader. But the trader will only be vulnerable if he or she opens the door to such experiences. The ego of a trader is fragile. Many things can affect it. The greatest of these is losses. As you know, many losses are unnecessary. If the reasons for losses are known and eliminated, then the ego will be protected and the many errors a trader can make due to emotional response of ego involvement will be eliminated, as well.

TAKE AN ASSESSMENT OF YOUR LOSSES ...
IT'S NOT TOO LATE!

Many of us feel that we are not achieving our true potential in the markets. We know that we are taking unnecessary losses. We know that we are not as disciplined as we should be. We know that we can do something to improve but we don't know what. The best thing to do is to begin learning from losses immediately. Begin the record- keeping approach I've described. If you're a newcomer to futures, or a veteran trader, get started on the right path immediately. It's not too late!

WHAT IF EVERYONE TOOK MY ADVICE?

There are, no doubt, many questions running through your mind about what I've stated in this chapter. You are probably thinking that the advice I've given is most elementary. Logically, if all traders follow it, there won't be many losers and the advice will self-destruct. This is not a logical conclusion.

If human beings were unemotional, and if human beings were perfectly disciplined, then there would be no markets. Inasmuch as emotion will always reign supreme when humans have money at stake, there will always be losers. The information is sound. It's the ability to put it into action with consistency and that differentiates success from failure.

SUMMARY

Many traders do not make the most of their losses. They assume that losses are the "cost of doing business" in futures trading, and they assume that a loss ends when it is taken. This is an incorrect assumption. Losses must be used as part the learning process. This chapter gave specific suggestions as to how one might benefit by keeping a record of profits and losses, and by implementing the knowledge of when, where and why losses were taken.

Chapter
20

Summing It All Up

What I have attempted to achieve in this book is bound to meet with praise and prejudice. Those who understand that the game of futures trading is not what it appears to be on the surface, but rather a test of behavior, discipline, emotion and skill, will truly appreciate the lessons this book has conveyed. To those who believe that to understand futures and to trade them successfully you need only acquire or develop a good system, this book will have been of no help. Those who have experienced the frustration of having a potentially successful trading system, yet not showing tangible benefits from its application may have found some important answers within these pages.

Ultimately, the true test of your learning and my teaching will be your ability to put the concepts and suggestions I have provided into successful action. For those who have already learned and internalized the directions and suggestions made in this book, the review will hopefully have proven valuable. Sometimes, as you know, it is necessary to learn and relearn lessons many times until they are truly learned. A lesson that must be relearned has not been learned.

Those who are, by their own lifestyle and *Weltanschauung,*

fixed in the mistaken belief that futures trading is based entirely upon knowing the facts will have learned otherwise in this book. Those who know that the facts of futures trading are of secondary importance to the issues of self-control, discipline, self-confidence and consistency will have found their beliefs and values strongly confirmed.

We are always tempted to search for better answers, better systems, better methods and better techniques. This search is the motivating force that drives the consumer to buy literally millions of dollars worth of computer hardware, software, charts, books, tapes, trading systems, seminars, etc. every year. In their eternal search for the external, most futures traders persistently ignore the value and importance of the internal. As you can tell by now, the emphasis of this book has been on the internal. Virtually everything I've said in the preceding chapters can be summarized by the following quotation from Lao Tzu:

> There is no need to run outside
> For better seeing,
> Nor to peer from a window. Rather abide
> At the center of your being;
> For the more you leave it, the less you learn.
> Search your heart and see
> If he is wise who takes each turn:
> The way to do is to be.[1]

In closing, my original temptation was to tell you that "My task has ended and yours just begun." However, this is not the case. My life and time in futures trading have made me understand that, no matter what my goals happen to be, I am always at the beginning of my task. Each challenge unfolds a task of greater importance and another step on the road to market mastery.

---

[1]Bynner, W. *The Way of Life According to Lao Tzu;* Capricorn 1944.

Epilogue

A Tale of
Two Traders

In the mayhem of the trading pits at the Chicago Board of Trade, where the life of a trader can be short and abysmal or long and prosperous, the fates and fortunes of many speculators, both private and public, have been molded. Here, in intense competition, traders are on the line virtually every second of the market day. Whether it be the Chicago Board of Trade, the Chicago Mercantile Exchange or the various New York exchanges, there is no better proving ground for the trader than the pits.

Very few individuals realize or appreciate what goes on when they place an order, or for that matter, what trading on the floor is really like. Several days on the floor will certainly go a long way in helping you gain respect for those who "beat their brains out" in this fierce game virtually every day. Yet, in spite of the pressure, the competition, the tension, and the challenge, the financial rewards are immense and they provide the motivation for the game to continue.

Here, in the pits, a tale of two traders has been born. The tale is a most interesting one indeed; but until the fact is brought to their attention, most people don't realize that the tale is a very instructive one for all traders, novice and advanced. What interests me most is that a great majority of the public, as well as many professionals within the futures industry have, until recently, been totally unaware of the tale which I am about to tell.

As you know, I have stated throughout this book that success in futures can be found on the extremes. Specifically, I indicated that whether technician or fundamentalist, short-term trader or long-term trader, futures trading can be a successful venture if you adhere to certain principles of trading, only a few of which are directly related to the system or systems you are using. Many of these principles are directly related to money management, trader discipline, persistence, consistency, risk management, etc.

One way to evaluate the validity of the concepts I have presented is to study the history of two pit traders at the Chicago Board of Trade, both on relatively opposite ends of the continuum, both immensely successful and both, until recently, relatively unknown to the public. By virtue of classic interviews with these individuals, we can gain many extremely valuable insights regarding the principles I've advanced in this book. The individuals to whom I refer are Tom Baldwin, known as the "biggest individual floor trader in Treasury bond futures" and J. Peter Steidlmayer, a 22-year veteran floor trader claimed to be "tremendously successful."

The material that follows is taken from interviews with Baldwin and Steidlmayer featured in *Intermarket*[1] magazine in February, March, June and July 1985. Specific reference notations are cited for your information. I urge you to read, study and assimilate both interviews in their entirety. Before taking a look at their different trading styles let's look at a brief biographical sketch of each trader.

---

[1]*Intermarket,* 175 W. Jackson, A621, Chicago, Ill., 60604.

TOM BALDWIN

According to *Intermarket*, Tom Baldwin, now about 30 years of age, began trading in the early 1980s. Starting with approximately $20,000, his net worth at the end of 1982 was $1 million. He has managed to parlay his starting amount in to "as much as $20 million" in several short years of trading. His trading is primarily short term.

He trades immense positions, often taking the opposite side of trades against large, well-known institutions, and on occasion trading as many of 6,000 T bond futures contracts per day. He concentrates on smaller moves with large positions. He frequently "breaks many rules" (to be illustrated later) thought to be sacrosanct by many traders. Though some have claimed that his success is merely "luck" and that he is headed for destruction, he has persisted. As stated in the *Intermarket* interview, "Baldwin is also known for his ability to operate calmly and to be right about the market direction more often than he is wrong..."

J. PETER STEIDLMAYER

By sharp contrast, J. Peter Steidlmayer is a 22-year veteran of futures trading at the Chicago Board of Trade. His approach to trading is based upon a specific theory of market behavior he calls the "Liquidity Data Bank.™" His wealth has been accumulated slowly and steadily over the years. He has traded through three decades of distinctly different markets, bullish, "choppy" and bearish and has succeeded in all. As you will see from what follows, Steidlmayer provides a marked contrast in many ways to Baldwin, yet though both men are on opposite ends of the continuum in many respects, they share success as well as many traits, attitudes and opinions that underscore and accentuate the value of everything I've attempted to teach you in this book. Let's look at a few comparisons.

The best way to compare the thinking, attitudes and opinions of Baldwin and Steidlmayer is to look at their comments regarding several important market issues, all of which have been discussed in considerable detail in preceding chapters. Their comments follow, taken verbatim from the interviews cited earlier, and listed under specific categories of importance. Study these in relation to what I've emphasized throughout the previous chapters:

TOM BALDWIN

RISK. Basically, my strategy is to reduce my risk. *I love trades that have minimal risk.* A trade with size and minimal risk allows tremendous profit.

IMPORTANCE OF THE TREND. That was the way I started making money. Most locals pride themselves in having no opinion of the market. But I ended up forced to have an opinion because I stood in an area of the pit that had less of a constant flow of paper, so it wasn't always easy to get in and out of trades. I needed a sense of where the market was going.

TECHNICAL VS FUNDAMENTAL APPROACH. I watch both factors, but I'm primarily a technician. I have to be. I have to know where the support and resistance levels are.

I also have to know what the fundamentals mean. Normally, though, the fundamentals occur outside of market hours, so I don't have the ability to capitalize on new information. During market hours all I'm able to do is utilize technical support and resistance levels.

IMPORTANCE OF DOING YOUR HOMEWORK. What kind of homework do you do?

Baldwin: I keep track of all the highs, lows and where the moving averages are. *It's real easy.* I can remember all the market highs and lows for a week. You have to remember what happened the last time we got down here or how the market behaved when it last rallied to this point.

Intermarket: Why is it that most of the people who are successful do their own homework?

Baldwin: If they love the business, then it's not work.

HISTORY REPEATS IN THE MARKETS. Usually the market tends to do the same thing over and over again—or *at least two or three times.* It tends to go up to a resistance point two or three times before it goes through it, and it also tends to go down to a support level two or three times before penetrating it.

THE VALUE OF BEING CONTRARY.

Intermarket: Do you like to buy the market when it approaches support trendlines?

Baldwin: No. I like to sell it there. If the market is able to go through it, it's all over. But it ends up that at the bottom I get long and at the top I get short. The reason: when the market seems strongest—when it may be at a top—large-sized orders come in to buy and the brokers look to me—and I sell to them. *You can't believe how much gets traded at the top and at the bottom of the market each day.*

Intermarket: And the largest amount you've lost in a day?

Baldwin: 10,000.

Intermarket: 10,000 ticks in one day? That's $312,500. How did that feel? Did you take a day off?

Baldwin: No. *I don't believe in that theory either.* I don't think that if you're in a slump, you have to get away.

CUTTING LOSSES AND ADMITTING YOU'RE WRONG.

Intermarket: What percentage of your entire net worth are you willing to lose in one day?

Baldwin: I'd set my limit at 10 percent. But I don't look at it as if I would lose it. My consoling thought at the end of a losing day is, "it's only 10 percent of my net worth."

CONTROLLING YOUR EMOTIONS.

Intermarket: Do you ever panic when you're losing big money?

Baldwin: No. Never. You lose too much money when you panic.

Intermarket: Is it that the least comfortable thing to do is the best strategy?

Baldwin: Frequently.

THE IMPORTANCE OF FUNDAMENTALS.

Intermarket: So the fundamental numbers really move the market?

Baldwin: Yes. Unless there's a major move in the market underway.

Intermarket: When we see a chart of the bond rally and how perfectly it fits into the trend lines—the geometric beauty, so to speak, how can a trader like yourself pay much credence to the fundamental numbers?

Baldwin: I look at the market as such: The technical aspects move the market during the day, and the fundamentals move it at night. Because very seldom does the trader have the chance to take advantage of a fundamental number during market hours. They come out at 7:30 (a.m.)

THE VALUE OF BEGINNING ON A SMALL SCALE.

Intermarket: A lot of people consider you the biggest local in the bond pit.

Baldwin: That changes. I have a theory on why traders reach certain levels. It's because everyone reaches a satisfaction level. *Everyone starts as a one-lot trader. Everyone should if they are to be successful.*

THE VALUE OF DISCIPLINE. I've learned discipline. I learned that at some point you have to say you're wrong.

VALUE OF THE TREND. Nobody's bigger than the market. I don't think many people really understand that philosophy. I think it's been proven time and time again. The market goes where it wants to go, no matter who's in the way or what's in the way. And that's why a person should trade 10 lots like one-lots.

THE IMPORTANCE OF QUICK ACTION AND AVOIDING HESITATION.

Intermarket: You know in advance where you'd like to buy and sell?

Baldwin: Usually. If what I thought was going to happen does happen, then I go. It just all of a sudden goes. I know it's right. I don't hesitate. If I hesitate, the opportunity is gone.

IGNORING THE OPINIONS OF OTHERS. But strangely, everyone thought it was the worst thing I ever did. They told me I was too new and couldn't do that. That they had never seen it done before by a novice. They scolded me and I agreed with them and told them that it was a one-time deal and will probably never happen again.

J. PETER STEIDLMAYER

Now let's take a look at some items from the Pete Steidlmayer interview. Take particular note of how the comments relate to what I've been preaching about throughout this book.

UNDERSTAND YOURSELF AND YOUR SYSTEM. They do not make good trading decisions. Generally, they have a poor trading strategy that asks too much of them. People fail at trading because they don't understand the market, they don't understand themselves and they don't understand the tools they're using.

THE INDIVIDUAL IS RESPONSIBLE FOR HIS OR HER OWN SUCCESS AND FAILURE. Success and failure in the marketplace have always been blamed on the market when in fact the blame belongs with the individual. Individuals will always defeat themselves.

THE IMPORTANCE OF CONTROLLING EMOTIONS. Most people make irrational or emotional decisions. Why is it that whenever you sell a house, you paint it first? It's because you know people make emotional decisions when buying, not decisions based on value. In all trading, you have to attach some semblance of value to the market. If you're trading below capacity at your operating level, you'll make nonemotional decisions. And like the market, and factories, a person's potential fluctuates. This ties into what I said about jealous people. Don't worry about the next guy's operating level. Don't worry about the richest guy in the pit or the guy who trades the most.

KNOW YOURSELF. "You" is something you have to know. You have to be you and you have to be satisfied with what you find. You can try to improve yourself, but you want to know your abilities and stay within them. You cannot be better than you normally are over time and your trading strategy has to reflect this. Most traders ask themselves to be at their peak potential all the time.

PRICE HISTORY OFTEN REPEATS.
Intermarket: So when you see a price recur over time . . .
Steidlmayer: You know that if the price is recurring over many time periods, it's facilitating the market's purpose of creating trade. Hence, if people are accepting it, that area of price activity represents value for that time frame. It's very important to know where this value area is.
Intermarket: So every day, you try to buy when the price is below the value area or sell when it's above it?

THE VALUE OF LIMITING RISK AND LOSSES. People feel that the more risk they take, the more they'll make. This is totally false. The more risk you take, the less you'll make. Where my knowledge and my approach have reduced my risk, it gives me a winning edge to the point that over a large sample size—1,000 trades or so—the result is a sure thing. I'm sure to make money. Think of it in terms of a used car. Everybody being equal, if you *know* that this car is worth $2,000, are you taking a big risk buying it for $1,000 at a bankruptcy sale? If you're a mechanic and you know it's worth that, you are taking virtually no risk. Yet you should make a very large return.

MAKE YOUR OWN DECISIONS. The most important thing in trading is to make your own decisions. Most people are cheating themselves by not making their own decisions.

THE IMPORTANCE OF SELF-CONFIDENCE. You need to have the information to *make your own decisions,* plus the confidence to make the adjustments that are called for. And unlike most traders, he doesn't try to predict where his shot is going to land. He doesn't care where it lands, because wherever it goes, he's going to handle it. He doesn't worry about it.

I'm no great golfer. So, I go up to the tee and worry. "I don't want to hit it in the trees, I don't want to hit it in the lake. What if I hook it?" I've got negative thoughts. Nicklaus goes up there, squares off, hits it, and wherever it lands, he hits it again. He's got confidence that he can handle the situation, no matter what happens.

It's the same thing in trading. When I'm trading well, I don't care if I have a monetary loss on, because I'm going to handle it. Nothing could ever hurt me, because I can handle whatever can happen.

DON'T TRY TO PREDICT TRENDS. If the person takes the usual approach to trading—charting and trying to predict the future—they have a 50% chance of being right or wrong.

SUCCESS CAN BE ACHIEVED BY THOSE WHO HAVE THE RIGHT APPROACH. The people who say that you can't make money trading are copping out. They don't have the ability to do it and so they knock it.

THE VALUE OF A GOOD PROFIT-TO-LOSS RATIO. I make 20

trades. I was right on only 12 of the 20 trades. I made $12,900 on the winning trades, my 8 losing trades totalled $1,800. I had a strong reason for most trades in the first place. So when I was wrong. I wasn't that wrong. *That's the real key to successful trading.*

CONSISTENCY AND ITS IMPORTANCE. Next, he doesn't shoot 64, then 78. He's consistent. He shoots 70, 69, 71 and so he's not riding an emotional rollercoaster. He's playing well within his capabilities.

I strongly suggest that you take the time to obtain and read both interviews. I think you will find these two interviews to be among the most instructive materials you will have ever read. As I said before, read them, assimilate them and study them.

Appendix

References and Reading List

Allen, R. C. *How to Use the Four-Day, Nine-Day, and 19-Day Moving Average to Earn Larger Profits from Commodities.* Chicago: Best Books, 1974.

Angell, George. *Computer-Proven Commodity Spreads.* Windsor, N.Y.: Brightwaters, 1981.

Angell, George and R. Earl Hadaday. *Spread Trading for the Risk-Conscious Speculator.* Pasadena, Calif.: Hadaday, 1979.

Angrist, Stanley W. *Sensible Speculating in Commodities.* New York: Simon & Schuster, 1972.

Appleman, Mark J. *The Winning Habit: How Your Personality Makes You a Winner or Loser in the Stock Market.* New York: McCall, 1970.

Arthur, Henry B. *Commodity Futures as a Business Management Tool.* Cambridge, Mass.: Harvard University Press, 1971.

Barnes, Robert M. *Taming the Pits: A Technical Approach to Commodity Trading.* New York: John Wiley & Sons, 1979.

Baruch, Bernard. *My Own Story.* New York: Holt, 1957.

Bernstein, Jacob. *Commodities Now through 1984.* Winnetka, Ill.: MBH Commodity, 1978.

Bernstein, Jacob. *The Handbook of Commodity Cycles: A Window on Time.* New York: John Wiley & Sons, 1982.

Bernstein, Jacob. *The Investor's Quotient.* New York: John Wiley & Sons, 1981.

Bernstein, Jacob. *MBH Seasonal Futures Charts a Study of Weekly Seasonal Tendencies in the Commodity Futures Markets.* Winnetka, Ill.: MBH Commodity, 1979.

Bernstein, Jacob. *Seasonal Chart Study 1953–1977, An Analysis of Seasonal Cash Commodity Price Tendencies.* Winnetka, Ill.: MBH Commodity, 1977.

Blumenthal, Earl. *Chart for Profit: Point & Figure Trading.* Larchmont, N.Y.: Investors Intelligence, 1975.

Bolton, A. Hamilton. *The Elliott Wave Principle: A Critical Appraisal.* Hamilton, Bermuda: Monetary Research, 1960.

Bynner, W. *The Way of Life According to Lao Tzu,* Capricorn, 1944.

Clasing, H. *The Dow Jones-Irwin Guide to Put and Call Options.* Homewood, Ill.: Dow Jones-Irwin, 1978.

Cycles. Foundation for the Study of Cycles. Pittsburgh, PA. January 1976.

Dahl, Dale C. and Jerome W. Hammond. *Market and Price Analysis, The Agricultural Industries.* New York: McGraw-Hill, 1977.

Dewey, Edward R. *Cycles, Selected Writings.* Pittsburgh, Foundation for the Study of Cycles, 1970.

Dewey, Edward R. *Cycles, the Mysterious Forces that Trigger Events.* New York: Hawthorne Books, 1971.

Dooley, Peter C. *Elementary Price Theory,* 2nd ed. Englewood Cliffs, N.J.: Prentice-Hall, 1973.

The Dow Jones Commodities Handbook: A Guide to Major Futures Markets. Princeton, N.J.: Dow Jones Books, 1983.

Dunn, D. and Hargitt, E. *Point and Figure Commodity Trading: A Computer Evaluation.* West Lafayette, Ind.: Dunn and Hargitt, 1971.

Elliot, R. N. *The Wave Principle.* New York: Elliot, 1938.

Esserman, Wayne. *Odds On Grain Spreading.* Delphi, Ind.: EWW Publishing, 1979.

Gann, William D. *The Basis of My Forecasting Method for Grain.* Pomeroy, Wash.: Lambert-Gann, 1970 (originally 1935).

Gann, William D. *Forecasting Grains by Time Cycles.* Pomeroy, Wash.: Lambert-Gann, 1976.

Gann, William D. *Forecasting Rules for Cotton.* Pomeroy, Wash.: Lambert-Gann, 1976.

Gann, William D. *Forecasting Rules for Gain-Geometric Angles.* Pomeroy, Wash.: Lambert-Gann, 1976.

Gann, William D. *How to Make Profits in Commodities,* Rev. ed. Pomeroy, Wash.: Lambert-Gann, 1951.

Gann, William D. *Forty-Five Years in Wall Street.* Pomeroy, Wash.: Lambert-Gann, 1949.

Gold, Gerald. *Modern Commodity Futures Trading,* 7th ed. New York: Commodity Research Bureau, 1975.

Goss, B. A. and B. S. Yamey. *The Economics of Futures Trading.* New York: John Wiley & Sons, 1976.

Granger, C. W. J. *Getting Started in London Commodities,* 2nd ed. Waterloo, Iowa: Investor Publications, 1975.

Harper, Henry H. *The Psychology of Speculation.* Burlington, Vt: Fraser, 1978.

Hieronymus, Thomas. *Economics of Futures Trading for Commercial and Personal Profit.* New York: Commodity Research Bureau, 1977.

Hieronymus, Thomas, A. *Economics of Futures Trading for Commercial and Personal Profit,* 2nd ed. New York: Commodity Research Bureau, 1977.

Hill, John R. *Scientific Interpretation of Bar Charts.* Hendersonville, N.C.: Commodity Research Institute, 1979.

Hill, John R. *Stock and Commodity Market Trend Trading by Advanced Technical Analysis.* Hendersonville, N.C.: Commodity Research Institute, 1977.

Horn, Frederick F. and Victor W. Farah. *Trading in Commodity Futures,* 2nd ed. New York: New York Institute of Finance, 1979.

Huff, Charles. *Commodity Speculation for Beginners: A Guide to the Futures Markets.* New York: Macmillan, 1980.

Hurst, J. M. *The Profit Magic of Stock Transaction Timing.* Englewood Cliffs, N.J.: Prentice-Hall, 1970.

Intermarket Magazine. 141 W. Jackson, Chicago, Ill. 60604.

Jiler, Harry, ed. *Forecasting Commodity Prices: How the Experts Analyze the Market.* New York: Commodity Research Bureau, 1975.

Kaufman, Perry J. *Commodity Trading Systems and Methods.* New York: John Wiley & Sons, 1978.

Kaufman, Perry J. *Technical Analysis in Commodities.* New York: John Wiley & Sons, 1980.

Keltner, C. W. *How to Make Money in Commodities.* Kansas City, Mo.: Keltner Statistical Service, 1960.

Kindleberger, Charles P. *Manias, Panics and Crashes: A History of Financial Crisis.* New York: Basic Books, 1978.

Kroll, Stanley and lrwin Shisko. *The Commodity Futures Market Guide.* New York: Harper & Row, 1973.

Lefevre, Edwin. *Reminiscences of a Stock Operator.* New York: American Research Council, 1923. Reprint ed., Burlington, Vt.: Books of Wall Street, 1980.

Leslie, Conrad. *Conrad Leslies Guide for Successful Speculating.* Chicago: Dartnell Press, 1970.

Levy, Haim and Marshall Sarnat. *Investment and Portfolio Analysis.* New York: John Wiley & Sons, 1972.

Lore, James H. and Mary Hamilton. *The Stock Market-Theories and Evidence.* Homewood, Ill.: Richard D. Irwin, 1973.

MacKay, Charles. *Extraordinary Popular Delusions and the Madness of Crowds.* London: L. C. Page, 1932.

McMillan, L. *Options as a Strategic Investment.* New York: Institute of Finance, 1980.

Oster, Merrill J. *Commodity Futures for Profit. . . A Farmer's Guide to Hedging.* Cedar Falls, Iowa: Investor Publications, 1979.

Oster, Merrill J. *Professional Hedging Handbook: A Guide to Hedging Crops and Livestock.* Cedar Falls, Iowa: Investor Publications, 1979.

Powers, Mark J. *Getting Started in Commodity Futures Trading,* 2nd ed. Cedar Falls, Iowa: Investor Publications, 1977.

Reinach, Anthony M. *The Fastest Game in Town: Trading Commodity Futures.* New York: Commodity Research Bureau, 1973.

Sharpe, William F. *Investments.* Englewood Cliffs, N.J.: Prentice-Hall, 1978.

Smith, A. *The Money Game.* New York: Random House, 1967.

Smith, Courtney. *Commodity Spread Analysis.* New York: John Wiley & Sons, 1982.

Teweles, Richard J., Charles V. Harlow, and Herbert L. Stone. *The Commodity Futures Game—Who Wins? Who Loses? Why?* 2nd ed. New York: McGraw-Hill, 1974.

Williams, Larry R. and Michelle Noseworthy. *Sure Thing Commodity Trading, How Seasonal Factors Influence Commodity Prices.* Brightwaters, N.Y.: Windsor, 1977.

Zieg, Kermit C., Jr. and Perry J. Kaufman. *Point and Figure Commodity Trading Techniques.* Larchmont, N.Y.: Investors Intelligence, 1975.

Zieg, Kermit C., Jr. and William E. Nix. *The Commodity Options Market: Dynamic Trading Strategies for Speculation and Commercial Hedging.* Homewood, Ill.: Dow Jones-Irwin, 1978.

Subject and
Author Index